Rev. Elbert R Collins

THE MAN WHO WAS RATZINGER

ALSO BY MICHAEL S. ROSE

Goodbye, Good Men

In Tiers of Glory

Priest

Ugly As Sin

The Renovation Manipulation

BENEDICT XVI

The Man Who Was Ratzinger

MICHAEL S. ROSE

SPENCE PUBLISHING COMPANY • DALLAS
2005

Published in the United States by
Spence Publishing Company
111 Cole Street
Dallas, Texas 75207

ISBN: 1-890626-63-5
978-1-890626-63-1
Library of Congress Control Number: 2005932992

Printed in the United States of America

A.M.D.G.

For
Barbara, Marcella, Madalena, Anna Maria, Salvatore,
and Numero Cinque

Contents

THE MAN WHO WAS RATZINGER

Stat crux dum volvitur orbis

A man with a definite belief always appears bizarre, because he does not change with the world; he has climbed into a fixed star, and the earth whizzes below him like a zoetrope.

G.K. Chesterton

A Different Kind of "Pendulum Papacy"

THE THOUGHT THAT, FOR SOME, was just too terrible to contemplate has become a reality. On April 19, 2005, the Sacred College of Cardinals voted to entrust the keys of St. Peter to Pope John Paul II's closest collaborator: Joseph Cardinal Ratzinger. "He has the most appalling reputation around the world as someone who has squashed theology and persecuted theologians," opined Margaret Hebblethwaite, England's leading Catholic feminist and a columnist for the *Tablet*. "He is the chief of the thought police, the master of the inquisition."[1] As the Vatican's long-time supreme custodian of doctrine, Cardinal Ratzinger was necessarily at the epicenter of many controversies involving the Catholic Church over the last two decades. His stellar defense of the faith in the face of opposition by radical feminists, homosexual activists, and secular fundamentalists is unparalleled in modern times. It is not surprising, then, that the election of Pope Benedict XVI has met with much gnashing of teeth among liberal pundits (and much cheering elsewhere).

The irony is rich: for years—decades, even—certain Church reformists of the Catholic Left like Hebblethwaite awaited the death of Pope John Paul II. Discontent with what they considered his conservative style of Church governance, they repetitiously contended that John Paul's successor would need to be more open to the winds of change in the world, willing to accommodate the desires of contemporary man. When it became clear that the Iron Pope was not going to give in easily to sickness or disease, the reformists pushed for an unprecedented papal resignation. The assumption was that once Karol Wojtyla was consigned to a Polish monastery, the Catholic Church would be primed for a "pendulum papacy." There is a saying: a fat Pope is always followed by a thin one, which is an oblique way of acknowledging that a new pontiff is invariably different—sometimes very different—from his immediate predecessor.

The reformists interpreted this adage to mean Karol Wojtyla would be followed by a man who would rubber-stamp their agenda to recast Catholic truths as negotiable planks of a political platform. The pendulum pope, it was hoped, would overturn the controversial moral stands taken by John Paul II. He would dispense with the discipline of priestly celibacy; he would permit the ordination of women, of gays, of lesbians. He would condone abortion and euthanasia, hand out condoms (especially in Africa), bless same-sex marriages, appoint accommodating liberal bishops, promote New Age spirituality, withdraw the indult for the traditional Latin Mass, and extol the virtues of folk liturgies and burlap banners.

Alas, it was not to be. In the words of dissident Swiss theologian Hans Küng, the election of Benedict XVI was "an enormous disappointment for all those who hoped for a reformist and pastoral pope."[2] Bernd Göhring, leader of the liberal German group "Church" put it more succinctly: "We consider the election of Ratzinger a catastrophe."[3]

In a manner of speaking, the reformists may get their "pendulum papacy" after all, but not on the terms they would have liked. To be sure, Benedict XVI has a great deal in common with his predecessor, but Joseph Ratzinger is certainly his own man, no mere pale reflection of the late pontiff. In fact, Benedict's papacy will likely be defined, not so much by its similarities with the previous pontificate, but by the contrast in its substance and style. No one doubts Benedict will uphold and defend the Catholic faith as did John Paul. There will be continuity in the papacy, but that continuity will likely come by way of translating the guiding lines of the Wojtyla pontificate into institutional reality. If his past history as Joseph Cardinal Ratzinger is any indication, Pope Benedict XVI is up to the task.

In the weeks and months before the death of John Paul, the future Pope Benedict consistently put forth an increasingly incisive analysis of serious problems facing the Church. He also revealed a bold plan for the future of the Church even before the conclave of 2005. Despite being the oldest pontiff elected in the past two hundred years, Pope Benedict XVI would seem destined to lead a consequential pontificate. This is, of course, what Church reformists and many others fear most. The election of the man who was Ratzinger, admitted Sister Joan Chittister, "has had all the force of a universal avalanche."[4]

The Besieged Soul of Christian Europe

In order to survive, Europe needs a critical acceptance of its Christian culture. Europe seems, in the very moment of its greatest success, to have become empty from the inside, as it were.

Joseph Cardinal Ratzinger[1]

As prefect of the Congregation for the Doctrine of the Faith for more than twenty-three years, Joseph Ratzinger viewed the Church and the world from a privileged vantage point. Consequently, Pope Benedict XVI is a man with a keen understanding of the many difficulties facing the Catholic Church today, especially in the West, where the faith is most obviously imperiled. In the same way Poland's Karol Wojytla was elected to save Christianity from militant atheism in Eastern Europe, Germany's *Panzerkar-*

dinal was tapped to face down the dangers of aggressive secularism and the increasing influence of Islam in Western Europe. Ratzinger is perhaps the one man left in the Church who is capable of surprising the world. At seventy-eight years old, he has not only wisdom and experience, but more important, the cultural and intellectual preparation to address these realities. If his past actions are any indication, he will do so by applying remedies that defy conventional wisdom and eschew the dictates of political correctness.

If any one point of reference can be taken as an augury of his papacy, it is Pope Benedict's clarion call to resist what he calls "the dictatorship of relativism." This has long been a particular concern of the new pope. In 1996, in an address to Latin American bishops in Guadalajara, Mexico, Cardinal Ratzinger said he believed that relativism has become the central problem for the faith.[2] He defines this prevailing philosophy as one that "recognizes nothing as definitive and leaves as the ultimate standard one's own personality and desires."[3] In other words, according to the relativist philosophy, people who disagree on moral and social issues can be equally right. In effect, relativists believe not in right and wrong but in accepting all beliefs, lifestyles, and moral systems—except, of course, those that question the concept of relativism. That's why relativists feel that they can freely criticize the pope and the Catholic Church, precisely because it condemns the relativist philosophy and all systems spawned by relativism. In his homily at the Mass that opened the conclave that elected him pope, Benedict XVI put it this way:

> How many winds of doctrine we have known in recent decades, how many ideological currents, how many ways of thinking . . . The small boat of thought of many Christians has often been tossed about by these waves—thrown from one extreme to the other: from Marxism to liberalism, even to libertinism; from collectivism to radical individualism; from atheism to a vague religious mysticism; from agnosticism to syncretism, and so forth. Every day new sects are created and what Saint Paul says about human trickery comes true, with cunning which tries to draw those into error.[4]

The Church, he insisted, must defend herself against threats such as "radical individualism" and "vague religious mysticism." During the same homily he also said that, "having a clear faith, based on the creed of the Church, is often labeled today as a fundamentalism. [. . .] Whereas relativism, which is letting oneself be tossed and swept along by every wind of teaching, looks like the only attitude acceptable to today's standards."[5]

This ideology that there are no absolute truths already dominates Europe and "constitutes the most radical contradiction, not only of Christianity, but also of religious and moral traditions of all humanity."[6] Consequently, atheists, agnostics, and nominal Christians (those who do not practice their faith in any discernable way) now form the majority on this once Christian continent. Western secularists have developed a culture that has succeeded in pushing God to the "the very fringe of society" and marginalizing the influence of Catholicism on politics and culture.[7] In excluding God, the Church, and the natural law, this "dictatorship" questions the foundations of any kind of absolute truth, any statement that transcendends the individual—whether it be in regards to social institutions, human sexuality or the definition of marriage. God and Church are no longer the arbiters of morals; it is rather the individual and his self-fulfillment that stands at the center of secular society.

The confirmation of this exclusion of God from public discourse came just months earlier, in 2004, when the European Union refused to acknowledge the continent's Christian roots in the preamble to its Constitution. Instead, it touted the non-religious influences of the pre-Christian ancients and the Enlightenment. Cardinal Ratzinger was a strong voice in the efforts by the Catholic Church and some political forces lobbying for such a simple mention in the new EU constitution. "When we talk about the Christian roots of Europe that does not mean everyone in Europe has to be Christian," he stressed, noting that while the history of Europe involved all the major religions, Christianity, Judaism and Islam, it was Christianity "that was the melting pot, the crucible" that allowed these elements to fuse.[8] The Vatican pushed for a concrete reference to the source of the values on which the European project is founded. As early as July of 2003, Pope John Paul II urged EU leaders to build the "new Europe" by revitalizing the continent's original Christian roots. "Europe has been widely and profoundly permeated by Christianity," he said in one of his Wednesday Angelus homilies. "The Christian faith has shaped the culture of Europe constituting a whole with its history and, notwithstanding the painful division between East and West, Christianity has become the religion of the European people."[9]

The Vatican was neither seeking a position of privilege for the Catholic Church in the European Union nor questioning the separation of church and state; it was merely attempting to safeguard the continent's common patrimony of values—values that could be used to unite the various European cultures. Nevertheless, some EU politicians reacted strongly to the Vatican's proposal. French President Jacques Chirac made it clear that he opposed any explicit mention of Christianity. "As the representative of a secular state, I am not in favor of religious references," he told a French newspaper.[10] Belgian Foreign Affairs Minister Louis Michel used stronger language. "This is absolutely unacceptable," he said of the Vatican's desire to see a reference to the Christian roots of Europe. "Secularism, or a clear separation of powers between the Church and the state, is a founding principle of the French republic that dates back to the 1789 revolution."[11] Columnist Joan Smith, writing in London's *Independent*, summed up the secularist mindset this way: "The EU is utterly godless. Let's keep it that way!" (Jan 23, 2003). Ironically, the European Union's founding fathers Robert Schuman, Konrad Adenauer, and Alcide de Gaspari were devout Catholic politicians who envisioned a unified Europe that stretched from the Atlantic to the Urals. Schuman (1886-1963), a former French Prime Minister, is even a candidate for beatification and his cause is well-advanced at the Vatican.

Other critics argued that an explicit mention of Christianity would offend the growing Muslim population in Europe, an argument that Cardinal Ratzinger found particularly flimsy and contrived. In a talk about the failed effort to Rome's Center for Political Orientation, the cardinal said he believed Muslims would have naturally expected Europe to affirm its religious patrimony, and the absence of any mention of religious faith tends to reinforce Islamic perceptions of Europe as a decadent society. "What offends Islam is the lack of reference to God, the arrogance of reason, which provokes fundamentalism," he said. "Europe was founded not on a geography, but on a common faith. We have to redefine what Europe is, and we cannot stop at positivism."[12]

Judging by the responses to the Vatican proposal, Ratzinger was correct. It wasn't Islam that was offended by the idea of identifying Europe with Christianity, but avowed proponents of European secularism, which Cardinal Jean-Louis Tauran defined as "nothing short of state atheism" (as opposed to "secularity," which simply means that the state does not establish any official religion). Cardinal Ratzinger repeatedly warned of this aggressive secular ideology that not only seeks to reject its Christian heritage, but more important, seeks to prevent Christian principles from influencing the "progress" of modern Europe. To that end, the future pope recognized nothing less than a totalitarian anti-Catholicism, one that aggressively tries to stifle the voice of the Church.

Cardinal Ratzinger called these reasons given in public debate superficial. "It is evident," he said, "that they disguise the true motivation more than they reveal it."[13] The true motivation, in the future pope's opinion, was that "according to secularist Enlightenment culture, Christian roots cannot be admitted into the definition of the foundation of Europe because these roots are dead, and they play no part in its present identity. This new identity, which is determined exclusively by the culture of Enlightenment, means that God has nothing to do with public life and with the basis of the state."[14]

Almost as if with the intention of proving the cardinal's point, the European parliament rejected the appointment of an openly Catholic politician on account of his "unacceptable" moral views. In the fall of 2004, José Manuel Durão Barroso, the incoming European Commission president, nominated Italy's Rocco Buttiglione as the European Union's next justice commissioner. Buttiglione, a professor of political science at Rome's St. Pius v University, was known as a close friend and counselor of Pope John Paul II and author of an intellectual biography of Karol Wojtyla. As a devout Roman Catholic, Buttiglione holds to the traditional teachings of the Church on sexual morality and has consistently taken a conservative position on political issues involving the dignity of life, opposing abortion and artificial insemination. He made the "mistake" of airing his traditional Christian views on women, homosexuality, and the family during a three-hour grilling by the parliament over his conservative religious and moral views.

"The family exists in order to allow women to have children and to have the protection of a male who takes care of them," Buttiglione said at his confirmation hearing. "This is the traditional vision of marriage that I defend."[15] His comment was interpreted by some as degrading to women, especially single mothers, and as a condemnation of "same-sex marriage," which has been legally recognized to some extent in European countries such as Sweden, Denmark, Germany, Belgium, the Netherlands, and most recently in Spain, until recent times a Catholic stronghold of Europe.

During his hearing Buttiglione also criticized the growing number of European women who put their careers before their families, pointing to the increasingly low birth rate in most EU countries, including Italy. The Catholic politician's most controversial statement, however, came when he was quizzed on his views of homosexuality. "I may think that homosexuality is a sin," he said, "but this has no effect on politics, unless I say that homosexuality is a crime." The European media widely characterized this remark as "crude." The influential BBC News even called it a "slur on gays."[16]

These traditional Christian views clearly rattled many of the European parliament. Buttiglione was denounced by some as unfit for the important post of Europe's justice commissioner. According to the logic of his detractors, since this position entails jurisdiction over issues of discrimination, including the rights of women and homosexuals, a man who operates according to a set of Catholic moral principles is wholly unfit to look out for the welfare and freedom of European citizens. Consequently, the nomination committee, in an unprecedented decision, rejected Buttiglione's nomination, citing the Italian politician's "extreme views."

What most commentators failed to point out is that Buttiglione's comments represent the widely held opinions of the mainstream Catholic electorate in his native country. The sort of comments he made at his confirmation hearing are in fact *de rigeur* for some politicians in Italy, where homosexual lobbyists have not yet gained the stronghold they have in some northern European nations. In sum, what the whole affair boils down to, as Bishop Joseph Duffy observed in the *Irish Independent*, is "pure intolerance."[17]

Jewish legal scholar J.H.H. Weiler refers to this type of religious antipathy towards believing Christians as "Christophobia"—an intense fear of Christian moral principles, especially on issues concerning life and human sexuality. The secularists in Europe have not only rejected their Christian identity—they hate it. For years now Ratzinger has contended directly and openly that Europe is sick with a pathological self-hatred—a disease in the realm of the human spirit. He blames this malaise partly on the modern concept of multiculturalism, which has helped sweep away the Christian foundations of Europe and allowed aggressive secularism to transform the cultural identity of the continent. The renowned French sociologist Daniele Hervieu-Leger coined the term "exculturation" to describe this phenomenon that has produced a continent of "new pagans" who live in a society now characterized by moral corruption and a materialistic view of the world.[18]

Just days before the death of his predecessor, Ratzinger warned Catholic leaders gathered at Subiaco, the cradle of Western monasticism, that the Church must react to this exculturation of Catholicism not by conforming herself to the times but by "bringing holy consternation, the gift of faith, the gift of friendship with Christ"—holding fast to the teachings of the Church and fighting the meteoric de-Christianization of culture.

In a landmark address to the Italian senate in May, 2004, Ratzinger outlined three areas in which he believes Europe must recover its Christian roots if it is to survive. The first is the natural law—recovering the unconditional status of human dignity before any civil jurisdiction. Fundamental, unchanging "rights" must be recognized and acknowledged as existing in their own right and therefore always deserving of respect by legislators. They are given by God and cannot be manipulated. Such a belief is in stark contrast to the secular relativist's view of "values" and "rights" in today's society. The second area is the status of the family, which Ratzinger calls the "basic cell" of Europe's social edifice. As such, the family is increasingly under attack by, among other things, the push for "same-sex marriage," an aggressive attempt to redefine the institution of marriage (and therefore, the family) in a way that not only offends the natural law, but common sense and the common good as well. The third is self-respect: "Our duty is to nurture in ourselves the respect before that which is sacred and to show the face of God who appears there—the God who has compassion on the poor and the weak."[19]

This three-point schema underscores Benedict's aversion to taking the path of accommodation and compromise as has been so often pursued in Europe since World War II. In fact, a strong case can be made that, in many European nations, the Church herself is partly responsible for its own exclusion from society, first by rejecting (or ignoring) its own rich religious patrimony and, second, by seeking to reinvent itself according to some new utopian pastoral model that was thought to be more palatable to modern Europeans. The result was a watered down faith—not merely a local problem here or there, but a generalized and systematic crisis.

The man who was Ratzinger appears not only well-prepared to resist the enticements from secular culture to water down Church teaching and to give into every passing social fad, he also appears prepared for the inevitable consequences of his efforts to purify the Church. Not a few wags have predicted that Ratzinger's militant *modus operandi* will drive milquetoast Catholics away. The new pope, however, recognizes that the Church cannot be reduced to a company with a product to sell and consumers to attract.

The maximization of the number of faithful is not Pope Benedict's strategic objective. In 1995, in the German edition of *Salt of the Earth*, a book-length interview with journalist Peter Seewald, Cardinal Ratzinger shocked the Catholic world by suggesting that it may need to disregard the notion of a "popular Church" that will be loved by everyone. He once wrote of the eighteenth-century Church, roiled by the Enlightenment, that it was "a Church reduced in size and diminished in social prestige, yet become fruitful from a new interior power, a power that released new formative forces for the individual and for society." Similarly, his governing metaphor for the short-term destiny of Catholicism is the mustard seed (Matthew 13:31-32), suggesting a much smaller presence but with a faith whose dimensions could move mountains. "Christianity might diminish into a barely discernable presence," he explained, because contemporary Europeans "do not want to bear the yoke of Christ."[20]

This statement, interpreted by the German press as a grim forecast, provoked a tempest in the cardinal's home country, amplified by exhaustive coverage of his remarks and his critics in the pages of *Der Spiegel*, Germany's leading news magazine. The future pope's "mustard seed Church" was interpreted as devastatingly controversial, yet the cardinal was simply acknowledging what is now taken for granted—that the Catholic Church in Europe was in catastrophic decline. There is no shortage of available statistics to support the contention. Judging by numbers alone, Catholicism has been withering from decades of steady erosion from the many forces of secularism.

Ratzinger envisions a "creative minority" capable of restoring religious vitality to Europe and beyond. Pope Benedict's objective is to sanctify souls through faith and grace. He believes that can be accomplished only by the reawakening of Christian identity in Europe, because it is in Europe where the "dictatorship of relativism" was born, and it is from Europe, through the homogenization of culture, that this dictatorship could get exported throughout the world. For this "reawakening" to succeed, Pope Benedict must necessarily capture the minds and hearts of Europe's youth—both children and young adults—in a very different way than his predecessor.

Pope John Paul obviously conveyed a genuine, personal liking for young people that was indisputably reciprocated. The problem, however, was that the vast majority of "John Paul youth" appreciated and revered the pope on a superficial level. Generally, even though hundreds of thousands of young men and women were attracted to the annual World Youth Days and other similar events, these festivities typically assumed the air of pop music gatherings at which the pope was treated more as a celebrity on the world stage rather than a moral and religious leader. Pope Benedict will need to do much more than that. He will need to equip young Catholics with a moral certainty and clarity to guide them through the culture wars that must necessarily continue to take place on the European continent if a reawakening of Christianity is to take hold in any meaningful and lasting way throughout the world. Placing his hopes on purely spiritual weapons in these battles, the pope's ultimate task is to steer the Church back to its fundamental mission, namely repentance and salvation. Given the relative superficiality of contemporary youth, the pope will need to address these issues in subtler ways: through the structures of Catholic education and catechesis, encyclicals directed specifically at young people in the context of the controversial issues of the day.

— 2 —

The "Ideology of Dialogue"

This mistaken notion of dialogue emphasizes not a search for objective and absolute truth, but a desire to put all religious beliefs on the same plane. And such dialogue gives rise to a "false idea of tolerance," which allows respect for other beliefs because it rejects the possibility of any objective truth.

Cardinal Joseph Ratzinger, 2000[1]

In foreseeing this "mustard seed" Christianity, Pope Benedict prefers the missionary impulse to timid dialogue with nonbelievers and those of other faiths—Christian and non-Christian. Here then may be the first significant difference between the German and Polish popes. As prefect for the Congregation for the Doctrine of the Faith, Cardinal Ratzinger differed with John Paul on several prominent issues, even the ones that most distinguished his twenty-six-year pontificate. The first of these differences came in regards to a 1986 interfaith meeting in Assisi. At John Paul's invitation, over one hundred representatives from the world's religions gathered in the city of St. Francis in order to pray side by side, "each to his own god."

On that occasion many of the Catholic churches in Assisi were temporarily given over to other faiths. African animists, Hindus, Jews, Shintoists, Jainists, Muslims, and a variety of Protestant sects conducted their own prayer services in consecrated Christian space. The Dalai Lama even set up an altar to Buddha in the local Church of St. Peter. Incense sticks set up on the tabernacle were burned in reverence of the Buddha. Cardinal Silvio Oddi, then prefect for the Vatican's Congregation for the Clergy, seventy-six years old at the time, observed: "On that day . . . I walked through Assisi . . . and I saw real profanations in some places of prayer. I saw Buddhists dancing around the altar upon which they placed Buddha in the place of Christ and then incensed it and showed it reverence. A Benedictine protested and the police took him away. . . . There was obvious confusion in the faces of the Catholics who were assisting at the ceremony."[2]

Although applauded by secularists who turned the event into a media showpiece, the pan-religious gathering released a torrent of criticism in many Catholic circles. According to reports in the Italian press at the time, Cardinal Ratzinger, who had predicted the confusion and foresaw the criticisms and "misinterpretations," declined to attend the event, distancing himself and his doctrinal congregation from what he saw as an ill-conceived token of good will. He feared that John Paul's egalitarian gesture would result in confusion about the Church's mission to propagate the Gospel of Christ throughout the world, transforming ecumenism and interreligious dialogue into a kind of syncretism in which every religion is understood as being as good as the next. This false ecumenism, Ratzinger knew well, was already systematically *de rigeur* among progressive Catholic theologians and formally denounced as heresy and in many Catholic dioceses throughout the world. The cardinal's criticism of his predecessor on this point was no secret. The Italian press reported that the future Pope Benedict saw Assisi as a further obfuscation of Christian identity.

In that same year, the Assisi gathering was accompanied by other controversial gestures by the pope in the name of ecumenism and interreligious dialogue. In February he allowed an Indian priestess to anoint his forehead with the *tika*, a red powdery paste the Hindus use as a sacred symbol to indicate recognition of the followers of the god Shiva. In March, on a visit to India, John Paul venerated the shrine of Mahatma Ghandi, calling the Buddhist political leader a "hero of humanity." These, along with other similar gestures (he also visited Buddhist temples, mosques, synagogues, and the Wailing Wall in Jerusalem), led many Catholics to believe that Catholicism was merely one of a number of salvific religions that worshipped the same vague God, seemingly nullifying the traditional Catholic teaching that no other religion can lead to salvation apart from Christ, the only "way, truth, and life." Even the Catholic bishops of India expressed alarm at the pope's speeches of "unprecedented openness" toward that country's majority religion. Bishop Andra Pradesh commented, "The Pope knows Hinduism from books, but we, who live with it and see the damage it does to our good people, would never make such speeches."[3]

Given the contagious fascination of Eastern mysticism and religious practices among Western Christians and post-Christians—this was one of Cardinal Ratzinger's enduring concerns—much of the Assisi proceedings were interpreted as an implicit endorsement of all the religions represented there that day. This was extremely troubling to many Catholics given that Vodou worshippers and tribal animists were included in what John Paul referred to specifically as the "great" religions.[4]

A few years earlier in *Redemptoris Hominis*, Pope John Paul II addressed the types of objections raised by Cardinal Ratzinger and other critics: "Some even express the opinion that [ecumenical and interreligious] efforts are harmful to the cause of the Gospel, are leading to a further rupture in the Church, are causing confusion of ideas in questions of faith and morals and are ending up with a specific indifferentism. It is perhaps a good thing that the spokesmen for these opinions should express their fears (no. 6)."[5]

In response to the mounting criticisms of the pan-religious summit, John Paul drafted *Redemptoris Missio*, which was published in 1990. The pope attempted to address the increasing lack of evangelizing missionary zeal, due in part to the "ideology of dialogue" with other religions that had become so popular since 1986. This encyclical was a candid acknowledgement that Cardinal Ratzinger's fears about religious relativism were justified. John Paul called this an "indifferent mentality, unfortunately widely diffused among Christians . . . which is rooted in incorrect theological views marked by a religious relativism that leads to the conviction that one religion is as good as another."[6] In effect, the "ideology of dialogue," where vague dialogue between believers of various faiths became an end in itself, a substitute for the missionary spirit that once fueled evangelization. Among theologians this ideology is undergirded by the new movement known as "religious pluralism"—in effect, the religious version of relativism.

In the Jubilee Year of 2000, it was Cardinal Ratzinger this time who released a document designed to dispel the escalating misunderstandings in this respect. Although it used many of the same citations founded in John Paul's 1990 encyclical, *Dominus Iesus: On the Unicity and Salvific Universality of Jesus Christ and the Church* emphasized more definitively and firmly that proclaiming the gospel of Jesus Christ to the ends of the earth is unavoidable and irreplaceable. At the news conference in which the document was introduced, Cardinal Ratzinger explained that *Dominus Iesus* was prompted primarily by three problems: First, the "worrisome influence" of Asian theologies, whose novelties were rapidly gaining popularity in the West. Second, the document was a necessary response to "the theology of religious pluralism" which is growing not only in theological circles, but also more generally in Catholic public opinion. Third, the cardinal said the document served to combat the "ideology of dialogue" that had come about as a result of serious misinterpretations of the teachings at the Second Vatican Council, especially from the documents *Nostrae Aetate* ("Of our age") and *Lumen Gentium* ("Light of the peoples"). "This mistaken notion of dialogue," Cardinal Ratzinger observed, "emphasizes not a search for objective and absolute truth, but a desire to put all religious beliefs on the same plane. And such dialogue gives rise to a 'false idea of tolerance,' which allows respect for other beliefs because it rejects the possibility of any objective truth."[7]

The document itself cites the error of some Catholic theologians who "have argued that all religions may be equally valid ways of salvation." It criticizes them for operating with "relativistic attitudes toward truth," which hold that what is true for some would not be true for others; for "subjectivism" which regards reason as the only source of knowledge; and "eclecticism," in which their theological research consists of uncritically absorbing ideas from a variety of philosophical and religious contexts that are incompatible with revealed and defined Christian truth.

The high-profile manner in which Cardinal Ratzinger presented the thirty-six-page document to the public underscored the seriousness of his concerns as supreme custodian of Catholic doctrine. He took some pains to emphasize that the document presented "nothing new," but was simply a restatement of timeless Church teaching that is to be held definitively by the faithful. The document reminded the faithful of the following essential points:

- Revelation in Christ is complete and cannot be complemented by teachings or practices of other religions;
- Although the Catholic Church rejects "nothing of what is true and holy in [non-Christian] religions," these other religions do not offer salvation apart from Christ and the Church;
- Only the canonical books of the Old and New Testaments are "inspired texts" because they were inspired by the Holy Spirit, have God as their author and teach without error the truth about God an salvation;
- The Holy Spirit is the spirit of the risen Christ, and "his action cannot be placed outside or alongside that of Christ";
- Protestant denominations have "defects" and cannot be considered "churches" in the proper sense; rather, they are "ecclesial communities";
- Prayers and rituals of other religions are not of "divine origin," and some contain "superstitions or other errors" that present obstacles to salvation;
- The Catholic Church is not a "sister church" to other Christian denominations, but a "mother";
- Other world religions are "gravely deficient";

- Catholics are obliged to proclaim "the necessity of conversion to Jesus Christ";
- The truths of the Catholic faith are not open to debate through "dialogue" with adherents of other religions;

Dominus Iesus was arguably the most controversial product of the John Paul pontificate and immediately received a deluge of criticism from within the Church. Progressive theologians involved in interreligious dialogue branded it a "pastoral disaster." In fact, much of the criticism made in response to the cardinal's document went a long way to prove the future Pope Benedict's point that confusion about interreligious dialogue and ecumenism abounds. Catholic critics said *Dominus Iesus* smacked of "cultural arrogance," and some suggested Cardinal Ratzinger had "an inadequate knowledge of parts of the world marked by religious diversity."[8] Pope Benedict's critics were, in effect, affirming that they did not think with the mind of the Church on these issues. They did in fact believe that dialogue was the ultimate goal of religion—if not dialogue as an end in itself, then dialogue in order to solve worldly problems—"to make communities safer, fairer, and more compassionate places to live,"[9] a very reductionist view of Catholicism.

Fr. John Prior, an English missionary, said he believed the "exclusivist 'absolute truth' language" of *Dominus Iesus* was not only offensive, but dangerous, suggesting it was certain to cause riots between Christians and members of other faiths from Northern Ireland to Indonesia.[10] Others simply saw it as "another club" that Ratzinger, the evil grand inquisitor, was using to beat theologians silly.

Even the upper echelons of the Church were divided over Cardinal Ratzinger's bold proclamation of these truths of the Catholic faith. Cardinals such as Milan's Carlo Maria Martini and Cardinal Edward Cassidy, at the time the president of the Pontifical Council for the Promotion of Christian Unity, believed the document would cause "communication problems" in the Church's ecumenical and interreligious relations. Martini dismissed the document as "theologically dense, peppered with quotations, and not easy to grasp."[11]

Dissident Swiss theologian Hans Küng, who had been disciplined by the Vatican in the past, characterized the document as "a mixture of medieval backwardness and Vatican megalomania."[12] Yet *Dominus Iesus*, penned by Ratzinger himself, has as its central message an essential Catholic truth that simply needed reiterating: "The thesis that the revelation of Jesus Christ is of a limited, incomplete, and imperfect character, and must be completed by the revelation present in other religions, is contrary to the faith of the Church.... This position radically contradicts the affirmations of faith according to which the full and complete revelation of the salvific mystery of God is given in Jesus Christ."[13]

Not a few critics contrasted *Dominus Iesus* with the "real world" actions of Pope John Paul II. An editorial in the *National Catholic Reporter* reminded readers of the pope's invitation to world religious leaders to meet for prayer at Assisi: "The pope asked no one to convert, insisted that no one accept Jesus—instead he reached out in humility, using the common language of penance and prayer. And in doing so, he dazzled the world. How do we reconcile that behavior with what is in *Dominus Iesus*?"[14] Cardinal Roger Mahony of Los Angeles and Bishop Joseph Fiorenza of Houston (president of the U.S bishops conference at the time) both invoked John Paul's irenic approach to the leaders of world religions at the 1986 pan-religious gathering in Assisi—in contrast to the perceived "rigidity" and "insulting nature" of Ratzinger's approach at the Congregation for the Doctrine of the Faith. Cardinal Mahony also suggested that *Dominus Iesus* "may not fully reflect the deeper understanding that has been achieved through ecumenical and interreligious dialogue over the last 30 years."[15] That suggestion was seconded by Archbishop Rembert Weakland, Milwaukee's outspoken prelate who was later disgraced by a sordid homosexual and embezzlement scandal. Weakland, a longtime proponent of the "ideology of dialogue" said many of his "dialogue partners" found the tone of Ratzinger's document "heavy, almost arrogant and condescending." The document "ignores all of the ecumenical dialogues of the last 35 years, as if they did not exist."[16] *Dominus Iesus*, of course, far from ignoring the dialogues of recent decades, actually sought to correct the fundamental nature of those dialogues.

The watershed document was received with equal rancor among the leaders of world religions who had been invited to Assisi four years before. Many felt slighted or insulted by the claim that the Catholic Church was the one, true salvific faith.

A symposium made up of prominent Christians and Jews that was to be held in Rome the week following the release of *Dominus Iesus* had to be cancelled after several Italian rabbis dropped out in protest over the document. Dr. George Carey, the former archbishop of Canterbury and head of the Anglican communion, mysteriously uttered nearly the same words as Archbishop Weakland in his formal response to Ratzinger's document. *Dominus Iesus*, he proclaimed, does not "fully reflect the deeper understanding that has been achieved through ecumenical dialogue and co-operation during the past thirty years."[17] He scoffed at the idea that the Anglican Church and other Christian denominations are not "proper churches" and charged that this particular statement "seems to question the considerable ecumenical gains we have made," suggesting that, through "dialogue," Anglican orders can become legitimate and valid in the eyes of the Catholic Church. "Of course, the Church of England," Carey added, "does not for one moment accept that its orders of ministry and Eucharist are deficient in any way."[18]

Just a few weeks after the release of the controversial document, Cardinal Ratzinger participated in a public debate with atheist philosopher Paolo Flores d'Arcais in a downtown Rome theater before a crowd of several hundred people. The question came up of the cardinal's claims in *Dominus Iesus* in relation to the Jews. When asked if he thought the Jews should acknowledge Jesus as the Messiah, he responded, "Yes, we believe that. That does not mean that we should force Christ upon them. The fact remains, however, that our Christian conviction is that Christ is also the messiah of Israel."[19]

Although *Dominus Iesus* was inarguably controversial and had more than its share of harsh critics, Cardinal Ratzinger's document was not without its supporters. Among the cardinals, Archbishop Giacomo Biffi of Bologna stood out by making the simple observation that the document rightly affirmed long-held Catholic truths: "This matter is of unprecedented gravity: in two thousand years it has never been necessary to recall and defend such elemental truths. Even within our [ecclesial] world orthodoxy seems to be threatened by hidden dangers from many sides."[20] Similarly, Archbishop Marcello Zago, secretary of the Vatican's Congregation of Peoples, observed that some Catholic theologians "have fallen into the danger" of watering down Christianity's claims about Christ and his Church in the interest of living peacefully alongside other religious believers. Zago, who worked as a missionary in Laos in the 1970s, acknowledged the necessity of *Dominus Iesus* in restating theological principles "forgotten" in particular regions of the world—not only in Asia, where the problem flourishes, but also in the United States and Europe, where these same problems can be readily found.[21]

Even the worries about *Dominus Iesus* becoming an "obstacle" to ecumenical dialogue amongst the various Christian denominations seems to have been overblown by critics. The leaders of the World Methodist Council, for example, actually welcomed the statement, saying they were delighted to see the Catholic Church affirm Jesus Christ as the one savior of the world. "In its continuing dialogue with the Roman Catholic Church, the World Methodist Council looks forward to further exploration on the question of how each partner can come to a fuller recognition of the churchly character of the other," the statement said. It added that they shared the Vatican's concern that Christians are interpreting religious pluralism to mean that every religion is of "equal significance."[22]

—

Pope John Paul II's last interreligious prayer gathering at Assisi came two years after the release of *Dominus Iesus*. The cardinal's influence on the "Pope of Dialogue" was obvious. The 2002 Assisi Day of Peace, ostensibly convened to pray for an end to the violence of terrorism, was noticeably different than the 1986 affair. The Vatican was careful on this occasion to prevent the obfuscation of Catholic belief and to prevent the perception that the pope was endorsing religious relativism. In a briefing to journalists, papal spokesman Joaquin Navarro-Valls emphasized that the meeting "is not an act of interreligious prayer. Thus, there is no danger of religious indifferentism or syncretism."[23]

This point was later clarified by Cardinal Ratzinger in his 2003 book *Truth and Tolerance*: "A distinction must be made between multireligious and interreligious prayer."[24] The prayers for peace offered at the Assisi gathering were presented by the Vatican as "multireligious"—all participants pray at the same time but in different places, in different ways, and to their own god or gods. According to Ratzinger, the participants "know that their own way of understanding the divinity and, therefore, their way of addressing it, is so different that a common prayer would be a fiction."[25] In contrast, he explained, "interreligious prayer" is when people of diverse religious beliefs pray together.

Is it possible for interreligious prayer to be truthful and honest? Ratzinger asks. In a word, he answers, "no." If Catholics participate in interreligious prayer services nevertheless, he adds in his book, it must be made clear that the prayer is to a personal God. The substance of the prayer must not be in contradiction to the *Pater Noster*, and it must be stressed that for Christians Jesus Christ is the sole redeemer of all people. This is, by the way, a much harder line than the one taken by Pope John Paul in his *Redemptoris Missio*, in which he recommends "prayer in common" as a way to "come closer to representatives of the non-Christian religions."[26]

Under the influence of Cardinal Ratzinger and the concerns outlined by *Dominus Iesus*, the Vatican took special care to avoid the appearance of relativism by taking precautions at the later Assisi gathering. The 2002 meeting differentiated itself from the 1986 pan-religious summit in one particularly striking way, one that served both to emphasize the "multireligious" (as opposed to "interreligious") nature of the prayer and to allay the type of harsh criticisms the first interfaith meeting inspired. Instead of holding non-Christian worship rituals in Catholic churches, the Vatican planners assigned each of the non-Catholic religions—Islam, Buddhism, Sikhism, African Animism, Hinduism, Tenrikyo, Shintoism, Judaism, Zoroastrianism, Janinism, and Confucianism—its own classroom in a convent school. These rooms were denuded of all Christian imagery—even the wall crucifixes were removed for the day. When the members of the various religions came together to talk about "peace," instead of meeting in the basilica, they convened beneath a big tent in the square.

Although Cardinal Ratzinger was not on the official list of attendees for the 2002 Assisi prayer summit, he was a last-minute addition to the program. This was taken to mean that he endorsed the revised Assisi conference, at least implicitly. Thus, the official line from the Vatican, with which Cardinal Ratzinger agreed, was that representatives of various world religions came together in Assisi to pray, but they did not "pray together" because they do not share the same faith, and in some cases do not even worship the same God.

The heart of the problem, according to Cardinal Ratzinger, is that false ecumenism and interreligious dialogue is just another part of the "dictatorship of relativism" in which truth becomes arbitrary and faith in Christ meaningless. This is not at all to say that Pope Benedict XVI will not pursue ecumenical and interreligious dialogue. In fact, in meetings with religious leaders of other faiths he has already given strong indications of his concern. Benedict's "dialogue," however, may well be of a very different sort than his predecessor's. The Ratzinger formula is based on the idea that authentic interreligious dialogue, by definition, neither promotes indifferentism nor allows "the relativistic misinterpretation of faith and prayer." That means widely misunderstood interreligious gestures, however sincere, will likely be relegated to the previous pontificate.

—

One aspect of interreligious dialogue that will likely come into play during the Ratzinger pontificate is securing the safety of Christians throughout the world. Christians who live in India, for example, are frequently victims of extremist Hindu aggression. India's laws, and those in certain other non-Christian countries, actually forbid the missionary activity of the Church, and punish it severely. Even in parts of the Orthodox world, Russia in particular, the Catholic Church is subject to an unacceptable bigotry and intolerance. Here then, there is truly a need for "dialogue."

— 3 —

Islam and the Crisis of Christian Identity

Europe is a cultural continent, not a geographical one. It is its culture that gives it a common identity. The roots that have formed it, that have permitted the formation of this continent, are those of Christianity.

Joseph Cardinal Ratzinger, 2004[1]

Pope John Paul II, who ordinarily spoke out courageously on all issues, ostensibly ignored the plight of persecuted Christians in Muslim countries. Christian populations continue to shrink in many of these nations due, in part, to long-term discrimination and repression by Muslim majorities. Catholic communities have been under physical attack by Muslims in recent years in Nigeria and the Sudan, in the Balkans and Chechnya, in Pakistan and the Philippines. At the same time, the growing Muslim community in Europe has been making increasingly aggressive religious demands. In 2004, for example, Muslims in the Spanish City of Cordoba asked for permission to pray inside the city's Catholic cathedral. Moreover, it is well documented that some Muslims view Europe and Christianity to be in decline and aspire to Islamicize the continent.

The Polish pope was criticized by some in the Church hierarchy for his rather laissez-faire attitude toward Muslim aggression and his romantic approach to Islam. He cultivated relationships with Muslims because he viewed Islam as an ally against Communism and the secular materialism of the West. He even forged a coalition with the despotic regimes of Iran, Libya, and the Sudan in order to oppose abortion advocacy at the 1994 UN conference on world population. This raised more than a few eyebrows, Cardinal Ratzinger's included. Writing in the *Arab News*, Amir Taheri observed that "Ratzinger believes that John Paul II's strategy of alliance with Islam has put the Vatican not on the side of the Muslim peoples, but on the side of despotic regimes that dominate the Muslim world."[2]

John Paul also appealed to what he called the "praying Islam" to control the rise of Islamic militancy and terrorism. While this seems reasonable at first glance, many critics found the appeal excessive. Renzo Guolo, author of *Xenophobes and Xenophiles*, defines this approach as "dialogue to the point of extremism," especially since Islam, unlike Catholicism, is "a religion without a center"—there is no Muslim hierarchy—and is unable to control the behavior of its faithful.[3] Cardinal Giacomo Biffi, Archbishop of Bologna, characterized the John Paul approach to Islam as Catholics "in favor of surrender."[4] Guolo characterizes the criticism this way: "By purifying the historical memory of the Church, asking forgiveness for the Crusades, and fawning upon the 'persecutors' of Christians, the pope, according to his critics, is exposing the Church to deep humiliation. Moreover, it transforms ecumenism into a sort of syncretism in which every religion is as good as the next."[5]

Vatican "outreach" to Muslims under John Paul II has also been criticized for diluting Catholicism and for not having yielded any benefits for beleaguered Catholic minorities in Muslim countries. Justo Lacunza Balda, head of the Pontifical Institute for Arab and Islamic Studies, a Vatican research group, said criticism also focused on "the lack of reciprocal goodwill gestures in many Muslim countries."[6] Consequently, many predict a radical change in the Vatican's strategy toward Islam and Islamist terrorism. "The era of de-facto appeasement under John Paul II is over," declared Joseph D'Hippolito in the *Jerusalem Post*. "The era of subtle, discreet, yet firm confrontation has begun." At Pope Benedict's inaugural Mass, for example, an unprecedented intercession for oppressed Christians was read aloud in Arabic.

There is little doubt that the relations between the Church and Islam will be at the heart of interreligious issues throughout Benedict's pontificate. In fact, the 115 cardinals who met to elect John Paul's successor cited the spread of Islam as one of the major issues facing the Church. The new Pope will necessarily avoid the symbolic gestures John Paul performed at his visit to the Omayyadi mosque (originally a Christian basilica) in Damascus, his kissing of the *Qur'an*, and his apologies for the Crusades, in favor of acting substantially. His motivation? First, in order to protect the Christian communities in the countries of the crescent moon and, second, to defend the Christian converts from Islam, who are routinely arrested even in "moderate Muslim" countries like Egypt and whose lives are threatened even in the secular countries of old Europe.

One objection that Ratzinger raised about Islamic culture is that its leaders tend to identify politics with religion, holding an almost complete disregard for religious freedom, and believing falsely that "only political power can make men moral." In a lengthy 2003 interview with the Italian daily *Il Giornale* he contrasted this belief with that of Christendom: "With Christ we find exactly the opposite position," he said. Christianity does not seek to unite "with any external power, political or military, but only with the power of the truth that convinces, the love that attracts."[7] The practical ramifications are many, but most importantly he insisted that converts to Christianity be treated respectfully in predominantly Muslim countries. A distinction between spiritual and temporal power would create "space for freedom, in which an individual can oppose the state" on issues of religion and worship, a condition that does not exist in many Islamic nations.[8]

Commenting in the Italian journal *La Civilta Cattolica*, Cardinal Ratzinger said, "We must have the courage to help these people," and get rid of a "certain Christian conscience that is unsure of itself."[9] He has also encouraged proselytizing Muslims, which has not been an operating principle among most Catholic missionaries who work with immigrant Muslim populations throughout Europe.

Judging from his previous writings and speeches, Pope Benedict is also not afraid to speak frankly about the threat posed to western civilization by the colonizing ambitions of Islam, ambitions that are not widely acknowledged by Westerners despite the growing body of evidence. Muslims, taking advantage of the welcoming governments of Europe, are immigrating to the continent en masse and taking over entire neighborhoods and cities, from England to Italy. While native Europeans are making substantial use of contraception and abortion to curb their own populations, the Muslims are doing neither. Statistics alone prove the point. The Muslim population in France doubled between 1989 and 1998, and if population trends continue, the eldest daughter of Christendom could have a Muslim majority by 2040.

In her bestselling book *Un crî dans le silence*, Brigitte Bardot attributed the "Islamicization" of France to her country's liberal immigration laws. "For twenty years we have submitted to a dangerous and uncontrolled underground infiltration," she wrote in 2003. "Not only does [Islam] fail to give way to our laws and customs. Quite the contrary, as time goes by it tries to impose its own law on us."[10] Noted Islam scholars such as Robert Spencer and Daniel Pipes have painstakingly documented this growing phenomenon. Spencer, for example, points out that not only is Islam—the *core* of Islam and not just "radical" Islam—incompatible with Western Christian culture, it is also incompatible with Western secular culture, probably even more so. Muslim cultural features such as arranged marriages, revenge killings, and female circumcision are diametrically opposed to Western values—both Christian and secular.

Europe's problem, then, can be boiled down to this warning that came from the late Dutch politician Pim Fortuyn: Muslims are exploiting the liberal Western political system, which guarantees them the right to free speech, well-being, and respect for religious rights, in order to ultimately impose their intolerant laws on that same Western society. Fortuyn, a leftist politician (although often referred to as a "far right-winger" due to his anti-immigration stance), was assassinated for making this very point, on the eve of the Dutch national elections in 2002.

Turkey's Catholic Archbishop Giuseppe Bernardini offered much the same caution. He warned that millions of Saudi petro-dollars have not been used to create work in the poor Islamic nations of North Africa or the Middle East. Rather, they have been used to build mosques and cultural centers in the heart of Christian countries with Islamic immigration, even including Rome, at the very heart of Christendom. How can we ignore this blatant Muslim program of "expansion and reconquest," asked the archbishop, especially when radical Muslims have been so forthright about their intentions? Bernardini recounted a conversation he had with a Muslim leader who said to him: "Thanks to your democratic laws, we will invade you. Thanks to our religious laws, we will dominate you."[11] In 2003 practically all of France's 1,200 mosques were funded by foreign governments, and out of the country's 230 major imams, none was French.[12]

—

The man who was Ratzinger is well aware that jihad terrorism and Muslim demographics threaten the survival of Christian (and secular) Europe. This is one reason why he publicly opposes Turkey's entrance into the European Union. European and U.S. leaders hail Turkey as one of the few, if not the only, "moderate" Muslim nation. Despite the fact that 80 percent of Turkey lies in Asia and the other 20 percent was taken over from Greece, they see Turkey's admittance to the EU as a political strategy, a way to isolate Islamic extremists by facilitating relations between Islam and Christianity. They apparently believe that denying Turkey's entry would risk handing it over to Islamic extremists and fundamentalists.

Proponents of EU status for Turkey reject the idea of a common European identity based on a common ancestry, religion, language, culture, and history. Rather, "European identity" means sharing common political values, a shared commitment to a liberal political system. The question for the vast majority of European politicians is whether Turkey is sufficiently secular, sufficiently feminist, sufficiently multicultural. But there is every reason to believe that the answer is still a resounding "no".

Ratzinger is one of the precious few churchmen who has dared to take issue with this popular European viewpoint. The cardinal took a broader, more historical view of Europe, careful to consider the various social, cultural, and religious forces that have shaped its identity over the past millennium. In pointing out the differences in these respects between old Europe and the Arab Muslim world, Cardinal Ratzinger called attention to the fact that most European nations are renouncing their own foundational Christian and cultural identity, noting that Europe risks becoming something quite alien. In an August 13, 2004 interview with the French magazine *Le Figaro*, Ratzinger argued that if a predominantly Muslim country of seventy million (more populous than France) were to become a member of the EU, it would "run counter to history." Reminding readers of the uncomfortable facts of history—the Turks seized Belgrade in 1521, laid siege to Vienna in 1529 after slaughtering the inhabitants of Pest (in Hungary), set fire to Moscow in 1573, and invaded Austria again in 1594 and 1683—he said:

> Europe is a cultural continent, not a geographical one. It is its culture that gives it a common identity. The roots that have formed it, that have permitted the formation of this continent, are those of Christianity. ... In this sense, throughout history Turkey has always represented another continent, in permanent contrast

> with Europe. There were the wars against the Byzantine empire, the fall of Constantinople, the Balkan wars, and the threat against Vienna and Austria. That is why I think it would be an error to equate the two continents. It would mean a loss of richness, the disappearance of culture for the sake of economic benefits. Turkey, which is considered a secular country but is founded upon Islam, could instead attempt to bring to life a cultural continent together with some neighboring Arab countries, and thus become the protagonist of a culture that would possess its own identity but would also share the great humanistic values that we should all acknowledge. This idea is not incompatible with close and friendly forms of association and collaboration with Europe, and would permit the development of unified strength in opposition to any form of fundamentalism.[13]

Little more than a month later, Cardinal Ratzinger reiterated his position, emphasizing that it was his *personal* view, in a lecture he delivered to the pastoral workers of his titular diocese of Velletri and was published in the Swiss newspaper *Il Giornale del Popolo*. He added the suggestion that Turkey itself would benefit more from an alliance with Muslim countries:

> Historically and culturally, Turkey has little in common with Europe; for this reason, it would be a great error to incorporate it into the European Union. It would be better for Turkey to become a bridge between Europe and the Arab world, or to form together with

> that world its own cultural continent. Europe is not a geographical concept, but a cultural one, formed in a sometimes conflictual historical process centered upon the Christian faith, and it is a matter of fact that the Ottoman empire was always in opposition to Europe. Even though Kemal Ataturk constructed a secular Turkey during the 1920s, the country remains the nucleus of the old Ottoman empire; it has an Islamic foundation, and is thus very different from Europe, which is a collection of secular states with Christian foundations, although today these countries seem to deny this without justification. Thus the entry of Turkey into the EU would be anti-historical.[14]

Around the same time, the Vatican released a document on the pastoral care of immigrants and migrant workers. Grounding itself in Ratzinger's view of "cultural identity" it warned of interfaith marriage, particularly cautioning Christian women of marrying Muslim men due to the religious and cultural consequences of such a decision. It was Ratzinger's interview with *Le Figaro* and his Velletri speech, however, that resounded around the world. Some rushed to judge the future pope as an anti-Muslim Christian supremacist. France's President Jacques Chirac, for example, countered Ratzinger's main claim by declaring that "the roots of Europe are as much Moslem as Christian"[15]—not only a patent absurdity, but a rather lame attempt to put the cardinal in his place. Others hailed Ratzinger for responsibly articulating what so many Europeans, and that includes Church leaders, wanted to say but the twin gods of political correctness and multiculturalism forbid. Some even wondered if Cardinal Ratzinger's comments signaled a movement of Vatican policy toward "isolationist retrenchment" in Europe.

In John Paul's Vatican, however, Ratzinger's opinion was in the minority and opposed to the official line from the Secretariat of State. Cardinal Angelo Sodano, content to pretend that the proposal presented no major obstacles, abstained from any official comment on the preliminary go-ahead given to Turkey's membership application by the European Commission on October 6, 2004. At that time, Sodano, acting in his official capacity for the Holy See, stated only that Turkey must respect democratic norms and guarantee more religious liberty, particularly for Christian minorities.[16] It is instructive to note that the Catholic Church and its property in Turkey are not yet dignified even by the most basic legal recognition.

The *New York Times* criticized Ratzinger's comments about Turkey's EU candidacy in a sharp editorial calling the future pope a "meddlesome cleric." It complained that "he and his fellow doctrinal conservatives worry about secularization and loss of Christianity, both of which are implied if Turkey joins the [European] union" and faulted the cardinal for placing his "personal values over universal values."[17] Upon his election to the papacy, the *New York Times*, reminiscing about the man who was Ratzinger, pointed out that "for all his doctrinal conservatism," John Paul II "was a man known for his outreach to people of other faiths."[18] It was feared that Benedict would not put so much effort into such "outreach" as his predecessor. For secularists, who believe that the primary function of a spiritual leader is not to act as a shepherd to the faithful but as a facilitator of "dialogue" with leaders of other religions, much seemed to be at stake.

European media outlets reacted in much the same way to the new pope's view of Turkey, overlooking that Ratzinger's comments were ultimately more a criticism of Europe than of Turkey or Islam. Reaction in Turkey was by far the most acute. Although Turkish prime minister Recep Tayyip Erdogan expressed his hope that Pope Benedict XVI "will soften his stiff opposition to Turkey's bid to join the [European] bloc," the Turkish media screamed displeasure over his election.[19] "The new pope is an opponent of Turkey," read the headlines on the front page of the daily *Sabah*.[20] The newspaper *Radikal* declared that Ratzinger "was Turkey's last choice."[21] Most of the Turkish media, however, missed one salient and possibly significant point. Ratzinger's predecessor in name, Pope Benedict XV, did so much to help Turkey during the First World War that a statue was erected in his honor in Istanbul, saluting the pontiff as "the benefactor of all people, irrespective of nationality or religion."[22]

Almost as if in anticipation of the objections the secularists and some Muslims would raise on account of his comments to *Le Figaro*, Pope Benedict addressed the very issue at the outset of his pontificate. In his first public Mass with the cardinals who elected him, the pope allayed some of the fear about his coming pontificate. "I welcome everybody with simplicity and love," he said, "to assure them that the Church wants to continue in open and sincere dialogue with [other faiths and cultures]."

Ratzinger's critics who accuse him of harboring anti-Muslim sentiments typically fail to acknowledge that Pope Benedict and the Church can engage in purposeful dialogue with Islam while seeking to shore up its Christian foundations. That is exactly what the new pope proposes.

—

Not only is Pope Benedict ready to defend Muslim aggression against minority Christian communities around the world, he is also willing to defend Muslim nations against unjust aggression from the West. When the U.S. led the 2003 invasion of Iraq, Cardinal Ratzinger expressed his opposition. Even before American soldiers were on Iraqi soil, he made it clear—along with Pope John Paul II—that the U.S. invasion was not morally justified. "It should never be the responsibility of just one nation to make decisions for the world, so we must still work with the UN. The fact that the United Nations is seeking the way to avoid war seems to me to demonstrate with enough evidence that the damage would be greater than the values one hopes to save."[23]

In an April 2003 interview with the Italian monthly *30 Giorno*, Cardinal Ratzinger clarified his position, which was shared by Pope John Paul II:

> [R]easons sufficient for unleashing a war against Iraq did not exist. First of all it was clear from the very beginning that proportion between the possible positive consequences and the sure negative effect of the conflict was not guaranteed. On the contrary, it seems clear that the negative consequences will be greater than anything positive that might be obtained. Without considering then that we must begin asking ourselves whether as things stand, with new weapons that cause destruction that goes well beyond the groups involved in the fight, it is still licit to allow that a "just war" might exist.[24]

Beyond being an explication of the practical application of the Church's "just war" theory, Cardinal Ratzinger's words also—significantly—speak of respect for the dignity of the human person without regard to race or creed as the highest Christian value. This is not only the new pope's personal conviction, it is also the teaching of the Church, one which Benedict XVI can be expected to vigorously uphold.

The man who was Ratzinger has also shown a sensitivity to the historical "culture" of Islam, another fact unfairly overlooked by his many critics. After the terrorist attacks on New York and Washington on September 11, 2001, Italian prime minister Silvio Berlusconi caused an uproar in Italy by claiming that Western culture is superior to Islam. Cardinal Ratzinger responded with an important clarification. "One cannot speak of the superiority of one culture over another," he told the Italian daily *La Repubblica*, "because history has shown that a society can change from one age to another."[25]

He suggested that at various times over the past several centuries, Islam has been superior to other cultures, having made enormous contributions to mathematics, philosophy, medicine and architecture. He added that at other times Christian culture has been superior. He did make a careful admission, however, that somewhat exonerated Berlusconi. He observed that in recent centuries Islam has undergone "forms of decadence" at a time when western culture was becoming more robust and energetic.

It is, of course, these various manifestations of Islam's "forms of decadence" with which Christendom and Pope Benedict XVI will have to contend in the immediate future.

— 4 —

The "Anti-Culture of Death"

In a world like the West, where money and wealth are the measure of all things, and where the model of the free market imposes its implacable laws on every aspect of life, authentic Catholic ethics now appears to many like an alien body from times long past.

Joseph Cardinal Ratzinger, 1985[1]

UNLIKE "CONSERVATIVE" POLITICIANS in the west, who are routinely accused of looking out for the rich and disregarding the needs of the poor—sometimes rightly accused—Pope Benedict's moral and religious conservatism transcends traditional political labels and stereotypes. In fact, Church teaching itself transcends the "conservative" versus "progressive" bipartisanship that defines American and European politics. The pope's world vision is much broader than that of a George W. Bush or a Margaret Thatcher. He sees no discrepancy, for example, between solidarity with the poor and opposing abortion and euthanasia, no discrepancy between opposing "pre-emptive wars" of American imperialism and supporting controls on mass emigration of Muslims to traditionally Christian nations.

The man who was Ratzinger has a good grasp of the materialism of the West, its perils and pitfalls. He also has a deep understanding of the suffering of the Third World, where Christianity strongly took root during the pontificate of John Paul II. Above all, Benedict does not want to see the Third World retreat into bourgeois forms of Christianity or be sucked into the Western vortex of moral relativism that would serve only to enslave the populations of Africa and Latin America in new ways.

One of the most frequently repeated canards during the interregnum period of 2005 was that John Paul's Vatican "brought us the spectacle of suffering and death" (as the *New Yorker* put it) in the Third World.[2] Media personalities, including certain priest commentators, suggested that the successor pontiff could end this reign of terror by promoting the use of condoms in AIDS-ridden Africa, and the use of birth control in the favelas and shantytowns of Central and South America. One Brazilian priest told the *New York Times*, "if I were pope, I would start a condom factory right in the Vatican."[3] Charges that the Church is responsible for the suffering of millions in

Africa were repeated over and over in hopes that the new Pope, whoever he might be, would buy in to the fallacious logic and change the teachings of the Church to accommodate sexual license. Contraception, especially the use of condoms, was given priority.

When the conclave elected Cardinal Ratzinger, commentators promptly shifted their ire onto the new pontiff. Pope Benedict XVI, they knew, would not fancy accommodationist solutions. Anglican Archbishop Desmond Tutu, for example, lashed out: "Benedict is a rigid conservative, who is out of step with the times. I had hoped for someone with a more reasonable position regarding condoms and HIV/AIDS."[4] Although Tutu's assessment of the new pope is skewed, he is correct to believe that the papal tradition of "insistent orthodoxy" will reign on. After his election, Pope Benedict made it clear that every pontiff must resist all attempts to "water down" Catholic teaching, but must rather link themselves and the Church to obedience to the word of God.[5] Joseph Ratzinger recognized the hackneyed condom solution for what it is: the furtherance of moral relativism, cultural imperialism, sexual libertinism and a surefire way to prolong the unfortunate suffering of entire continents. Nevertheless, the fallacy still remains. Is the Church really responsible for the suffering and death of millions on the African continent? Is the Church really responsible for the spread of AIDS?

Critics contend that if the Church were to sanction the morality of contraception, millions—it's always "millions"—of lives would be saved. Such logic goes a long way in proving the relativist mentality of contemporary Westerners. Contraception and homosexual acts are not immoral because the pope says so. The Church pronounces contraception and homosexual acts immoral because they are objectively sinful. In the case of AIDS in Africa, even if Pope Benedict were to somehow "repeal" the Church's teaching on contraception in the hope that persons infected by HIV could have "safe sex" with uninfected partners, as many or more Africans would die from the disease.

The fact is that, thanks to Western "family planning" organizations, condoms are already being distributed—and presumably used—by the millions throughout African nations. Nevertheless, condoms have not been working to stem the AIDS epidemic on the continent. The opposite is true: condoms have been a significant factor contributing to the spread of the disease for the simple reason that condoms are, at most hopeful estimates, only 90 percent effective against the transmission of the HIV virus.[6] With a false sense of security, many African men and women engage in unsafe sex practices precisely because they believe that they are protected against the disease by the use of condoms. Statistics bear this out. The March 2004 issue of *Studies In Family Planning* examined the topic in an article entitled "Condom Promotion for AIDS prevention in the Developing World: Is It Working?" The answer was a resounding "no."[7] In fact, according to statistics examined over the previous decade, the nations with the highest rate of condom availability—South Africa, Kenya, Botswana and Zimbabwe—have the highest rates of HIV infection.

On the other hand, Uganda, the country with the lowest rate of condom availability has by far the lowest incidence of AIDS in its country. Uganda once had the highest rate of AIDS prevalence in the world. Starting in the late 1980s, however, the Ugandan government chose to use a different approach to the disease than that of other African nations. Instead of handing out condoms and encouraging HIV/AIDS patients to use them, Uganda promoted abstinence before marriage and fidelity after marriage. In this country that chose the path recommended by the Catholic Church, from 1991 to 2001 the incidence of AIDS in the population dropped from 15 percent to 5 percent. Compare that to the countries that focused on condom distribution: Botswana rose to 38 percent and Zimbabwe to 32 percent by 2001 and has risen even higher since then.[8] Though very few people seem to realize it, it's obvious that the Church, and especially the pope, have been set up as the bogeyman in this affair.

Benedict's measure of the truth is not the misplaced compassion of condom promoters or the moral relativism of contraception advocates; it is Christ and the Gospel. The pope's plan of action is grounded in the corporal and spiritual works of mercy, which must become part of the renewed identity of the Christian nations of the Western world if they are going to be able to assist the poorer countries of the developing world. Benedict has already called attention to the poorest nations by pointing out that too many Catholics in North America and Europe are self-centered and obsessed by their own pet political interests, such as "gay rights," "reproductive rights," "ordination rights," and so forth. Rich nations, he has said, too often seek solutions that really only serve as expedient ways to export the most decadent aspects of Western culture—condoms, for example.

This, of course, is not a new interest of the pope's. In a May 13, 2004, address to Italian politicians, Cardinal Ratzinger spoke of "the God who has compassion for the poor and the weak, for the widows and orphans, and the stranger; of the God who is so human that he himself became a man, a man of suffering, who, suffering together with us, gives to pain dignity and hope."[9]

Just a few weeks after his election, in his first meeting with the clergy of Rome, Pope Benedict drove this point home with a stern criticism of colonialism, charging that Europe has too often brought corruption and violence to the African continent: "We have to confess that Europe has exported not only faith in Christ, but also all sorts of vices, the sense of corruption, and violence that devastates" the continent. In response to a question posed by an African priest working in the Diocese of Rome, he made it clear that European Christians have a grave responsibility to see to it that along with faith there be found the strength to resist the vices and to create a "happy Christian Africa."[10]

In fact, it is obvious that the subject is dear to the new pope. He devoted his first series of Wednesday catechetical talks at St. Peter's to the problems of the richer nations, especially in relation to those of the developing world. Christians, he said, should beware of the "false idols" of riches, power, prestige, and the easy life. He cautioned against the ambitions that men are tempted to regard as "the high points of life," involving the pursuit of worldly power and material goods. The believer, he said, must not allow those temptations to deflect his attention from God.[11] Christians should rather renounce power and wealth and instead serve others using the humility of Christ as their example: Even though Jesus was equal to God, He did not exploit His power and use it "as an instrument of triumph, sign of distance or expression of crushing supremacy," the Pope said on another occasion.[12]

Ironically, the same commentators who believe that Pope Benedict should speak loudly in favor of mass distribution of condoms criticize the pope when he speaks out against the ill uses of Western power and wealth. "Social justice" comments such as these ought to have been welcomed, coming as they did just prior to a G-8 summit. But campaigners for a shift in the balance of global wealth towards the poor uniformly denounced the pope, claiming that the head of one of the world's richest and powerful institutions cannot properly pronounce on the vices of avarice and greed. In effect, they were admitting that, for them, sexual license trumps matters of social justice.

It is the "power," the influence, and the authority of the papacy that bothers them more than the person of Joseph Ratzinger, whether they are willing to admit it or not. Critics are angered, for example, that the Vatican has a seat, as an observer nation (like Switzerland), at the United Nations and has used that position to protect the dignity of the human person by scuttling the worst proposals put forth at Population Summit in Rio de Janeiro and the World Conference on the Rights of Women in Beijing.

Of course, the same people who accuse the Vatican of terrorizing the Third World are also offended by the Church's stands on basic life issues—abortion, contraception, and euthanasia. Their rhetoric is at times as fantastic as it is illogical. Adele M. Stan, writing in the *American Prospect*, charged that Cardinal Ratzinger, as prefect of the Congregation for the Doctrine of the Faith, waged a "cunning campaign against all those 'Kumbaya-singing' nuns, priests, prelates, and theologians who dared take issue with the most draconian of the Church's doctrines: those that condemned women to a life of biological destiny."[13] Though she doesn't explain why the cardinal's "campaign" was "cunning," it is clear that she takes issue—in the typical manner of the Western secular journalist—with the Church's protection of human life from conception to death.

John Paul was a towering giant when it came to confronting the "culture of death," another by-product of the dictatorship of relativism. In his installation Mass as bishop of Rome at the Cathedral of St. John Lateran, Pope Benedict made it clear that "life" will be a key word in his pontificate. "Freedom to kill is not a true freedom," he said in reference to the commonplace practice of abortion, "but a tyranny that reduces the human being into slavery."

The basic life issues form an important part of the crisis of morality which the Church and the world face today. Back in 1985 when Cardinal Ratzinger granted Italian journalist Vittorio Messori a book-length interview that was published as *The Ratzinger Report*, he spoke of the "drama of morality" and the "culture of permissivism" that had become the model of many influential Western nations such as the United States. In this context, he pointed out, it is difficult if not impossible to present Catholic morality as reasonable. With money and wealth as the measure of all things, Catholic morality appears "as a kind of meteorite which is in opposition, not only to the concrete habits of life, but also to the way of thinking underlying them"[14] This condition is most obvious when it comes to the fundamental issues of life, family, and human sexuality—issues which are often intertwined.

In speaking of a "series of ruptures," Cardinal Ratzinger prophetically warned against the logical consequences of the contraception mentality. Two decades have passed since the cardinal issued this stern caution, and it is instructive to note that all the consequences he detailed have come to pass. The "ruptures" he spoke of are, first, a rupture between sexuality and marriage, and, second, a rupture between sexuality and procreation. "Separated from motherhood, sex has remained without a locus and has lost its point of reference: it is a kind of drifting mine, a problem and at the same time an omnipresent power."[15] The result: self-indulgence and licentiousness, wherein the sexual libido becomes the only possible reference point of sexuality: "Everyone is free to give to his personal libido the content considered suitable for himself. Hence, it naturally follows that all forms of sexual gratification are transformed into the 'rights' of the individual. Thus, to cite an especially current example, homosexuality becomes an inalienable right. (Given the aforementioned premises, how can one deny it?) On the contrary, its full recognition appears to be an aspect of human liberation."[16]

From this flows the "anti-culture of death," a term coined by Cardinal Ratzinger and often used by Pope John Paul II. This anti-culture entails not only sexuality without procreation (that is, contraception and homosexuality), but procreation without sexuality. This biological manipulation of man can be seen in the "increasingly shocking medical-technical experiments so prevalent in our day": human cloning, embryonic stem cell research, genetic engineering, sex-selective abortions, and in-vitro fertilization. All of these technologies have become the hot-button bioethics issues of the twnety-first century. But such "biological manipulation" doesn't stop there. The medical-technical experimentation continues and now even includes human cross-breeding.

For example, a group of researchers from California's Stanford University is creating mice with human brains, using stem cells of aborted babies, in the hope that the hybrid human-mice might lead to a cure for diseases such as Parkinson's and Alzheimer's. Professor Irving Weissman, who heads Stanford's Institute of Cancer/Stem Cell Biology admitted that there is no way of knowing beforehand whether human-mice will develop human characteristics such as improved memory or problem-solving ability.[17] Opponents of the plan are concerned that the human stem cells could migrate to other parts of the animals, creating human sperm or eggs in their reproductive system. Should two such human-mice mate, it could create a human embryo trapped within a mouse's womb. If that sounds far-fetched, consider that in the United Kingdom, the nation's parliamentary committee on science and technology recommended giving the go-ahead to allow the experimental implantation of human embryos into animals. The report argued that "new technologies should be used until harm is proved." Committee member Dr. Evan Harris responded to critics of the report by arguing that it is more ethical to permit research on a "chimera," an embryo which is half-human half-animal, than it is to permit research on fully human embryos.[18]

There are also other consequences to what Cardinal Ratzinger considers this "retrograde moralism," the most pernicious of which is abortion. He elaborated in *The Ratzinger Report*: "Fecundity separated from marriage based on a life-long fidelity turns from being a blessing (as it was understood in every culture) into its opposite: that is to say a threat to the free development of the 'individual's right to happiness.' Thus abortion, institutionalized, free and socially guaranteed, becomes another 'right,' another form of liberation."[19]

To underscore the importance Pope Benedict XVI places on the inviolability of human life from conception to death, he immediately preached in defense of life. At his installation in the Basilica of St. John Lateran on May 7, 2005, the pope reiterated that it was his solemn duty to proclaim this inviolability even in the face of "all efforts apparently intended for the benefit of the human person, and in the face of erroneous interpretations of freedom."

The pope acted on these words in the first month of his pontificate. In an address to the Italian bishops conference, he praised the prelates in their efforts to oppose a national referendum intended to overturn key provisions in a law passed the previous year on medically-assisted fertility, known in Italy as "artificial procreation." The law bans donations of sperm and eggs, defines life as beginning at conception, and allows fertility treatment only to "stable heterosexual couples" who are living together and can prove infertility. According to the referendum initiated at the request of abortion rights groups, voters were asked to vote "yes" to four questions jettisoning articles which give unborn babies (referred to as "embryos") the same rights as "born babies," limit to three the number of eggs that can be harvested and fertilized at any one time, give couples the right to resort to a donor, and end the ban on embryo research. The referendum had the support of all Italy's major daily newspapers, as well as the Leftist Democrat party, the heirs of the Italian Communists.

Pope Benedict and the Italian bishops called on voters to abstain from voting on the June 12, 2005, referendum; if less than 50 percent of registered voters failed to turn out for the referendum, it would be declared invalid. Proponents of the referendum were angry at the pope's "interference" in Italian politics, despite the fact that Benedict did not address his appeal to the Italians alone, but to the world, and not only to Catholics, but to all men of good will. In the Church's judgment, reiterated by the pope, the inviolability of unborn life is not simply a commandment of the Christian faith, but a natural law written on the hearts of all men.

The results of the referendum were overwhelming. Only 25.5 percent of registered Italian voters turned out to vote, rendering the referendum null and void. Of those who did vote, 22 percent still voted against the referendum.[20] This translates into the lowest voting participation in the entire history of the Italian republic and a smashing victory for Pope Benedict XVI, the Catholic Church and, of course, unborn babies.

In typical fashion, those who disagree with the moral vision of the Catholic Church asserted that the pope had no "right" to engage in political lobbying. Communist politician Franco Giordano, for example, in an interview with Italy's Radio Radicale, called the pope's remarks an "unwarranted interference in the affairs of the Italian state."[21] Also among those who lashed at out at Pope Benedict was Italy's minister for equal opportunities, Stefania Prestigiacomo. Calling the Catholic Church's views "misogynist," she accused the pope of disregarding the "health" of women.[22] Daniele Capezzone went so far to call the pope's remarks "an unprecedented attack which is aimed at putting Italian democracy under the auspices of the Vatican."[23] What Pope Benedict had actually said to the Italian bishops was that it was their duty to "illuminate and motivate Catholics and all citizens in the imminent referendum on assisted procreation."[24]

This was not the first time that Joseph Ratzinger was falsely accused of interfering in the politics of a nation on the issue of inviolability of life. Senator John F. Kerry, the Democratic nominee for president of the United States in 2004, was well known for his consistent public support of abortion. He also presented himself as a Catholic in good standing, attended Mass on Sunday, and received Holy Communion each week, despite rejecting one of the most fundamental Catholic teachings: the right to be born.

In a bold move in the months before the U.S. election in 2004, Cardinal Ratzinger sent a memo to Cardinal Theodore McCarrick of Washington, D.C. His strongly worded note established a principle of refusing Holy Communion to those politicians who have taken public stands in favor of abortion. Although Senator Kerry was not mentioned by name, the implication was obvious. The cardinal's letter was addressed to McCarrick not only because he was head of the "domestic policy" committee for the U.S. bishops, but because as archbishop of Washington he often dealt directly with Catholic politicians, including Senator Kerry.

The memo was intended to be a confidential communication between the Vatican and the U.S. bishops. It was leaked, however, to the Italian newspaper *L'Espresso*. The message was clear:

> The practice of indiscriminately presenting oneself to receive Holy Communion, merely as a consequence of being at Mass, is an abuse that must be corrected.... Regarding the grave sin of abortion or euthanasia, when a person's formal cooperation becomes manifest (understood, in the case of a Catholic politician, as his consistently campaigning and voting for permissive abortion and euthanasia laws), his Pastor should meet with him, instructing him about the Church's teaching, informing him that he is not to present himself for Holy Communion until he brings to an end the objective situation of sin, and warning him he will otherwise be denied the Eucharist.[25]

Despite the clearly worded statement by the future pope, the U.S. bishops came to a different conclusion at their semi-annual June meeting in 2004, just months before the November election. Cardinal McCarrick, speaking to the bishops gathered in Denver, appointed himself the spokesman of the concern that "the sacred nature of the Eucharist might be turned into a partisan political battleground."[26] Cardinal McCarrick also told the bishops that the Holy See trusted in the responsibility of the American bishops to judge on their own whether refusing Communion to public and obstinate sinners is a "pastorally wise and prudent" decision, despite the fact that the cardinal's memorandum hinted at no such "trust."

After days of heated discussion between a vocal minority of U.S. bishops (Archbishop Raymond Burke and Bishop Michael Sheriden in particular), who supported Cardinal Ratzinger's instruction, and the vast majority, who wanted to bury the prefect's words, the U.S. bishops conference issued a statement that contradicted Cardinal Ratzinger. Entitled "Catholics in Political Life," the document left it up to each individual bishop the decision of whether to give Communion to pro-abortion Catholic politicians. The statement passed 183 to 6, indicating a sharply felt chasm between the courage and conviction of the future Pope Benedict and the vast majority of the U.S. bishops. It remains to be seen whether the U.S. bishops will continue down this same path throughout the Ratzinger papacy.

— 5 —

Expelling the Filth, Purifying the Church

How much filth there is in the Church, even among those who, by virtue of their priesthood, ought to belong entirely to Christ! How much vainglory, how much self-complacency!

Joseph Cardinal Ratzinger, 2005[1]

ANOTHER DISTINGUISHING MARK of John Paul II's pontificate was his penchant for issuing *mea culpas* for what he called the "dark pages" of Church history. He publicly apologized for the Church's culpability ninety-four times—to the indigenous peoples in the Dominican Republic in 1984, to Muslims in 1985, to Jews and Africans in 1986, and to the Greek Orthodox in 2001, among others. Wojtyla's "theology of apology," as it was dubbed, was generally received with applause by the worldwide media, although it was mingled with harsh criticism of the Catholic Church for doing too little, too late. Some of the pope's harshest critics on this issue, however, could be found among the cardinals, especially inside the Vatican. The most prominent, though not the most vocal of these critics (Cardinal Giacomo Biffi wins that distinction) was Cardinal Ratzinger, who worried that these apologies would be misinterpreted in much the same way as was the 1986 interfaith meeting at Assisi.

Although it is doubtful that Pope Benedict will continue these gestures of public self-flagellation for the past sins of the Church, that doesn't mean the new pope will not be issuing any apologies. In fact, in the month before he was elected to the See of Peter he did just that. In his Good Friday meditations on the Stations of the Cross at the Roman Coliseum, he asked for forgiveness not for the Church's past faults, but for those of today. Moreover, he asked forgiveness from God, not from the world. In an obvious reference to the abuse scandals that have dominated the Church in recent years, he made this intercession: "Lord, your Church often seems like a boat about to sink, a boat taking in water from every side. In your field we see more weeds than wheat. To see the vesture and visage of Your Church so filthy throws us into confusion. Yet it is we ourselves who have soiled them! It is we who betray you time and again, after all our lofty words and grand gestures. Have mercy on your Church."[2]

Throughout these meditations, Cardinal Ratzinger made several references to a necessary purification of the Church, and it seems safe to say that the new pope sees this "purification" as a central task of his pontificate, one which he believes needs to begin with his priests and bishops. Reflecting on Jesus' third fall under the weight of the Cross he prayed, "How much filth there is in the Church, even among those who, by virtue of their priesthood, ought to belong entirely to Christ! How much vainglory, how much self-complacency!"[3]

A few days after the white smoke appeared above the Sistine Chapel, the Italian newspaper *La Stampa* published an article about a document that was making the rounds among the cardinals the week prior to the conclave. Although it was unsigned, Cardinal Ratzinger is believed to have been the author. According to *La Stampa*, the document detailed a wide variety of problems inside the Church. Most significantly, it provided a detailed portrait of the situation of the clergy around the world, and particularly in Europe and North America: "The 'lack of integrity' of too many priests is put in stark relief: violation of the rules of celibacy, obviously, but not only that; problems tied to money, problems with the use of the faithful's contributions, and problems concerning the confessional as well."[4]

The most obvious problem of "filth" in the Church is that of the widespread clergy abuse scandals in the United States and other nations. Shortly after the election of Joseph Ratzinger, Cardinal Francis E. George of Chicago was widely quoted regarding a brief meeting he had with the future pope about the scandal in the U.S. church. Cardinal George commented that Ratzinger seemed to have a "good grasp of the situation."[5] Two days later when George kissed the ring of the newly elected pontiff, Benedict told the American cardinal, speaking in English, that he remembered the conversation the two men had had, and that he would attend to the situation.

In 2002, however, Cardinal Ratzinger was criticized for a comment he made on the sensitive subject. "In the Church, priests also are sinners," he said during a visit to Spain. "But I am personally convinced that the constant presence in the press of the sins of Catholic priests, especially in the United States, is a planned campaign, as the percentage of these offenses among priests is not higher than in other categories, and perhaps it is even lower."[6] At first blush the comment seems ill-conceived for someone so well-informed as Cardinal Ratzinger. One interpretation suggests that he was referring to the fact that the American secular media readily promotes sexual sins, homosexuality, and the gay subculture, and in many ways has long covered up the sexual abuse of minors by Catholic priests precisely because these priests were predominately homosexual.

A more probable explanation is that, through his work directly examining abuse cases at the Congregation for the Doctrine of the Faith, he later came to understand the extent of the problem and its damage. In the intervening years, Ratzinger had more responsibility than any other churchman for deciding how to discipline priests accused of sexual abuse. As the cases came across his desk by the dozens, he learned that the problem was broader and deeper than he could have ever imagined. According to Msgr. Charles J. Scicluna, a Maltese priest who was one of Cardinal Ratzinger's closest collaborators at the Congregation for the Doctrine of the Faith, "reading through the hurt this misconduct creates was obviously a great source of spiritual and moral suffering."[7] For one reason or another, the cardinal underwent some sort of conversion of thinking on the matter. One thing, however, is certain. Upon his election to the papacy, the Holy Father was aware of the clergy sex abuse problem, spoke openly of the "filth" in the priesthood, and promised to attend to the problem.

Ironically, though, the Western media ignored the pope's remarks in the interest of making Pope Benedict the new bogeyman of the sex abuse crisis. He was accused of being no less than a grand conspirator and even named in a lawsuit as part of far-fetched racketeering claim. Hundreds of news articles were spawned by a report in the left-leaning *Sunday Observer*, published by *London's Guardian* newspaper.[8]

The *Observer* contended that Cardinal Ratzinger was a key player—if not *the* key player—in covering up the Church's clergy sex abuse scandal. The evidence presented was a confidential letter sent to the bishops of the world in May of 2001. According to the *Observer*, the future pope reminded the bishops of the "strict penalties facing those who referred allegations of sexual abuse against priests to outside authorities . . . [Cardinal Ratzinger's letter] urged them to investigate such allegations 'in the most secretive way . . . restrained by a perpetual silence . . . and everyone . . . is to observe the strictest secret which is commonly regarded as a secret of the Holy Office . . . under the penalty of excommunication."[9] The article quoted various American "campaigners" supporting the *Observer*'s conclusion that Ratzinger showed "he was prepared to use every means possible to ensure that abuse allegations were not investigated by authorities outside the Church."[10]

Three men from Houston, Texas, used this same May 2001 letter written by then-Cardinal Ratzinger as the basis for a lawsuit against the Catholic Church. The men claim that when they were twelve and thirteen years old, they were molested at St. Francis de Sales Church in southwest Houston in 1995.[11] They accused Juan Carlos Patino-Arango, a seminarian at Houston's St. Mary's Seminary of the alleged abuse. According to the Archdiocese of Houston, when the allegations first arose against the seminarian, he was expelled and Child Protective Services was contacted. Patino-Arango then returned to his home country of Colombia. The men are suing the archdiocese and Archbishop Joseph Fiorenza. They added Pope Benedict to the lawsuit, saying they believed the letter is proof that Ratzinger obstructed justice and was a co-conspirator in keeping claims of sex abuse secret.

Although various media reports characterized the letter as "secret" or "confidential," it had long been posted on the Vatican's website in its original language, Latin, along with several translations, including one in English. It had also been published in hardcopy back in 2001 in the *Acta Apostolicae Sedis*, the official journal of the Holy See. Edward N. Peters, an American canon lawyer, characterized the press reports on the Ratzinger letter as "much ado about not much."[12] The letter, in fact, was written to clear up some confusion surrounding "certain procedural questions among canonists as to which canonical crimes were 'reserved' to the Congregation for the Doctrine of the Faith," Peters explained, "that is, which ecclesiastical offenses are considered serious enough that Rome itself would adjudicate the case." He also noted that the letter was not written solely about the subject of sexual abuse, but all "ecclesiastical crimes," most of which are not crimes under criminal law, for instance, breaking the seal of confession. "Secrecy," Peters explained, is essential to due process because it protects the integrity of the investigation, shields the victims from unwanted exposure and protects the accused, especially the wrongly accused—the same sort of procedures carried out by civil authorities conducting criminal investigations. But most important, nothing in Cardinal Ratzinger's 2001 letter prevents or discourages victims or their parents from going to the police, to private attorneys, or even to the press with their stories.

Contrary to the portrait painted by the *Observer* and other media outlets who followed its lead, Judge Ann Burke, a self-proclaimed liberal Catholic, said she was very optimistic that Pope Benedict XVI would move to address the problem of clergy sex abuse in the United States. Burke was at one time head of the U.S. Bishops' National Review Board of Clergy Sex Abuse. In an interview with CBS television news she explained that she and other members of the board traveled to Rome in January, 2004 to meet with Cardinal Ratzinger and to offer Vatican officials the "full story" and scope of the abuse problem. Ratzinger spent three hours with the American group. Two months later, in a March 2004 letter, Cardinal Ratzinger echoed the National Review Board's suggestions that bishops examine their role in the scandal. "What better position can we be in the Catholic Church today?" Judge Burke asked. "To know that the Pope read [the report], talked to us and followed through."[13] She also said she believed her meeting with the future pontiff laid the groundwork for Ratzinger's conversation with Cardinal George.

Perhaps in fulfillment of his promise to Cardinal George, Pope Benedict selected William J. Levada, San Francisco's archbishop, as his successor as prefect of the Congregation for the Doctrine of the Faith. Levada is one of four bishops in the United States responsible for the effort against clergy sex abuse. Twenty-four years before the election of Pope Benedict XVI, the archbishop briefly worked for Cardinal Ratzinger at the Congregation for the Doctrine of the Faith and is said to be "old friends" with the new pontiff—surely a man Pope Benedict feels he can trust in such an important Vatican position.

Nevertheless, given Cardinal Ratzinger's obvious concern for doctrine and for dealing with the epidemic of clergy sex abuse, the appointment of Archbishop Levada strikes many as a poor choice. Aside from the San Francisco prelate's personal connections to the man who was Ratzinger, Archbishop Levada's reputation precedes him. Far from being seen as the kind of stalwart "enforcer" that Ratzinger was, he is known in the United States as a moderate compromiser and protector of a notorious disgraced bishop. In fact, in an interview with the *San Francisco Chronicle* he referred to himself as a "cocker spaniel," in contrast to the popular caricature of Joseph Ratzinger as "God's Rottweiler."[14]

As archbishop of San Francisco, Levada capitulated on the issue of providing mandatory healthcare to same-sex partners of diocesan employees, casting his compromising stance not as an endorsement of homosexuality, as many people saw it, but as support for "increasing benefits" for health care coverage. Mayor Willie Brown had passed a city ordinance that requires any business or agency doing business with the City of San Francisco to offer to domestic partners the same benefits it offers to spouses. Levada defended his decision in a 1997 article in Father Richard John Neuhaus's journal *First Things*. He argued that, given the context of debate and considering that San Francisco has the highest per capita homosexual population in the country, he did not feel that opposing the ordinance would be worth the lengthy court battle that would necessarily ensue.[15]

Archbishop Levada also allowed the rector of St. Patrick's Seminary in Menlo Park to write articles in support of same-sex unions. Fr. Gerald Coleman, who wrote regularly for Levada's diocesan newspaper, was known as a staunch supporter of homosexual rights. "Some homosexual persons," wrote Coleman in one column, "have shown that it is possible to enter into long-term, committed and loving relationships, named by certain segments of our society as domestic partnership . . . I see no moral reason why civil law could not in some fashion recognize these faithful and loving unions with clear and specified benefits."[16]

Archbishop Levada, however, is most commonly criticized for his role in the clergy sex abuse scandal in the United States. Far from appearing as someone who understands the roots of the scandal—predatory homosexuality and gay cronyism in the priesthood—he has been criticized by prominent personalities as enabling the cover-up. For example, in 2001, Archbishop Levada appointed James Jenkins to head a local Independent Review Board in response to a series of clergy sex abuse scandals in northern California. Jenkins, a clinical psychologist, served nearly three years on the panel before resigning. In his resignation letter to Levada he accused the Archdiocese of San Francisco of "deception, manipulation and control" for refusing to release the panel's findings on sexual abuse allegations involving forty priests. He told the archbishop that the panel risks being reduced to "an elaborate public relations scheme," and doubts that the archdiocese could restore public trust "given its present leadership and the state of its corruption."[17]

In the late 1990s Levada was also accused of leaving a priest in ministry despite credible allegations and a civil lawsuit against him. Levada was also accused of retaliating against Fr. John Conley, the priest who reported to police the priest in question, whom he suspected had molested a fifteen-year-old altar boy at the parish. Archbishop Levada removed Conley from active ministry for accusing his pastor, Fr. James Aylward, of sexual misconduct. Conley was stripped of his priestly faculties and banished to a retreat center. According to court documents, long after Fr. Aylward admitted fondling teenage boys for his sexual gratification, Archbishop Levada admitted that under the same circumstances he would not have reported Aylward to police as Fr. Conley had done. Investigative reporter Ron Russell, writing for *S.F. Weekly* summed up the case: "Following Conley's accusations, Levada ordered the priest not to refer to Aylward as a 'pedophile' and not to mention the matter to nuns assigned to St. Catherine's Parish, where Aylward was pastor and Conley served as an associate priest. Levada quietly transferred Aylward to a parish in Mill Valley. The pastor was later ushered into retirement after—to the humiliation of archdiocese officials who had defended him while vilifying Conley—he admitted sexual misconduct."[18]

Michael Guta, the attorney who deposed Archbishop Levada, had this to say about the San Francisco prelate: "Given the influential role he has assumed within the church on the sex abuse issue, he appears to have a high tolerance for alleged sexual misconduct involving priests. I found it disturbing then, and I find it disturbing now."[19]

As part of a court settlement with Fr. Conley, Levada had to apologize to the mistreated whistleblower and admit that the priest had in fact acted properly in turning Aylward into police. The Archdiocese of San Francisco also paid $750,000 to the parents of the altar boy who had been sexually abused by Fr. Aylward.

Archbishop Levada's support and protection of Bishop Patrick Ziemann also raises questions. In 1999, Ziemann resigned as Bishop of Santa Rosa, California, after admitting to sexually exploiting a young Costa Rican man he brought to the diocese and ordained despite the fact that the priest had not completed seminary training and could barely speak English. (He had been kicked out of seminaries in Honduras, Mexico, and New Jersey before meeting Ziemann.) After Bishop Ziemann discovered that Fr. Jorge Hume Salas had been stealing money from the collection plate at his parish, the bishop began to extort sex from the priest in exchange for not taking criminal action against him. The bishop had the young priest wear a beeper so that he could be summoned at the bishop's whim to engage in sexual activities in cars, hotel rooms, and even in the Santa Rosa chancery offices. In other words, Bishop Ziemann forced the priest into an ongoing non-consenting abusive sexual relationship.

Despite the revelations about Ziemann's sordid relationship with Fr. Hume Salas, as well as the bishop's financial irresponsibility which left his diocese in millions of dollars of debt, Archbishop Levada lauded his episcopal friend to the bitter end. The day Bishop Ziemann resigned, after an audio tape surfaced exposing the bishop's sexual exploits, Levada extolled his friend as someone who had done much to help the diocese.[20]

After the resignation, Levada stepped in as administrator of the Santa Rosa diocese for a year, until a new bishop was appointed. During that time Levada discouraged police and prosecutors from pursuing criminal charges against Bishop Ziemann. Archbishop Levada also quietly settled a civil lawsuit with Fr. Hume Salas for $535,000, while swearing the priest to secrecy. Since that time, more men have come forward to accuse Bishop Ziemann of sexual abuse, including one man who contends that the Santa Rosa bishop paid him for sex for nearly two decades.[21]

The bottom line on Archbishop Levada, then, is that his many critics from California accuse him of being more interested in quelling scandal and protecting clergy sex abusers than in pursuing justice. Expelling the filth and purifying the Church is already going to be a very difficult task for Pope Benedict, but with Archbishop Levada as the prefect of the Vatican congregation that is expected to deal with the clergy sex abuse problem, it is going to especially difficult.

To Levada's credit, his first major act as the prefect for the Congregation of the Doctrine of the Faith was to issue a decree that effectively banned a well-known founder of a religious order from public ministry. On May 27, 2005, the CDF issued the decree, signed by Levada and approved by Pope Benedict, against seventy-three-year-old Fr. Gino Burresi, founder of the Congregation of the Servants of the Immaculate Heart of Mary. Although the decree cites abuses of the seal of the confessional and spiritual direction, Vatican sources have said that another motive for taking action against the Italian priest was credible accusations of sexual abuse with young adult seminarians under his guidance.[22] The accusations dated back to the 1970s and 1980s.

The lengthy report prepared by the CDF under Ratzinger and issued alongside the 2005 decree by Levada cites a 1989 commission of cardinals formed to examine allegations against Fr. Burresi. The commission urged the CDF to take action against Fr. Burresi because if it did not, the Vatican's silence would be interpreted by his followers as evidence of unfair hostility against the popular priest: "[Fr. Burresi's followers said] 'that the Secretariat of State defends Fr. Gino [Burresi], thus victory is assured.' If no new limitation is applied to his ministerial liberty simply due to the fact that the proven offenses have been prescribed [by the statute of limitations], probably the sentence of this court will be used as an instrument of propaganda in favor of the accused. He will be able to continue to do harm to those psychologically weak persons who place themselves under his spiritual direction."[23]

— 6 —

The Invention of a "Culture of Homophobia"

Increasing numbers of people today, even within the Church, are bringing enormous pressure to bear on the Church to accept the homosexual condition as though it were not disordered and to condone homosexual activity.

Joseph Cardinal Ratzinger, 1986[1]

THE POPE KNOWS ONLY TOO WELL that he can't begin to expel the filth from the ranks of the clergy without addressing the issue of homosexuality, and in particular, the crisis of homosexual priests. Given that Cardinal Ratzinger has already tackled this hot-button issue in an authoritative way more than any churchman who has ever lived, there is legitimate cause for hope.

To be sure, the man who was Ratzinger was despised, above all, by radical homosexual activists. Their disappointment and rage over the new pontiff cannot be understated. Political pundit Andrew Sullivan, who never misses an opportunity to present himself as "gay" and "Catholic" in the same sentence, shuddered at the election of Benedict XVI. "We're back in the 19th century," he lamented. "Those of us who are struggling against what our Church is becoming, and the repressive priorities it is embracing, can only contemplate a form of despair."[2] *Time* magazine gave Sullivan space for an extended denunciation of the man who was Ratzinger. Calling the new pope a "creature of the 20th century opposed to the modern world," Sullivan wrote that "for a struggling gay Catholic like me [reading Joseph Ratzinger] is like reading a completely circular, self-enclosed system that is as beautiful at times as it is maddeningly immune to reasoned query. The dogmatism is astonishing."[3] It is exactly "dogma" to which Sullivan objects, and he has voiced his clamorous objections for years.

Sullivan was by no means the most vociferous of the homosexualist critics. In the weeks immediately following the April conclave, the mainstream media and the "gay press" produced a record number of articles filled with intemperate quotes from homosexual lobbyists. For Kara Speltz, co-chair of the Catholic division of Soul Force, an ecumenical homosexual advocacy group, the election of Ratzinger was her worst nightmare. "Personally," she said, "I don't know if I can stay in a church with a Nazi in the papacy."[4] Mark Jordon, a homosexual Catholic theologian who once taught at the University of Notre Dame, said the election made him sick to his stomach. Jordon, whose books include The *Invention of Sodomy in Christian Theology* and *The Silence of Sodom: Homosexuality in Modern Catholicism*, worried that his days might be numbered as a Catholic theologian. "I felt kicked in the stomach," he said of Pope Benedict's election, "and then I probably felt kicked out the door."[5] Sam Sinnett, president of Dignity USA, a Catholic homosexual advocacy group that was banned from Church property by Cardinal Ratzinger in 1986 for undermining Church teaching on human sexuality, said he felt "a profound betrayal by the leaders of the Roman Catholic Church."[6]

The Gay Lesbian Alliance Against Defamation (GLAAD), for their part, called on the American media to examine "Ratzinger's documented rhetoric and writings related to gays and lesbians," suggesting that the new pope has been on a decade's long campaign to vilify gays and lesbians.[7] GLAAD's advice was heeded by major U.S. news outlets, which portrayed Ratzinger as "virulently anti-gay."[8]

Some of his most strident critics, however, have been among the Catholic clergy and those in the Catholic Church involved in "ministry to homosexuals"—which is now known by its more inclusive name of "ministry to the LGBT community." (LGBT is used to denote "lesbian, gay, bisexual, and transgendered.") Reginald Cawcutt, an auxiliary bishop in Cape Town, South Africa, had some particularly bitter words to say about the Vatican's doctrinal chief. In 1999, an Illinois-based lay activist group called Roman Catholic Faithful exposed a website and internet discussion group for "gay priests and seminarians." Called St. Sebastian's Angels, it featured graphic male pornography, including a "pulsating penis" on its entry screen, and lurid discussion and graphic descriptions of homosexual activities and other elements of the clerical gay subculture. Many of the messages were explicit in their condemnation of Catholic Church teachings regarding human sexuality. Bishop Cawcutt was the so-called "episcopal advisor" to the group—in an unofficial capacity, of course.[9] On the website, the South African bishop expressed the hope that Cardinal Ratzinger would be poisoned. He and other members of the group accused the prefect of conducting a "witch hunt" against homosexually active priests, actually recommending that the future Pope Benedict XVI be sodomized by some of them.

Ironically, those who accused Cardinal Ratzinger of being on a "sexual witch hunt" for defending Catholic teaching, have actually engaged in a witch hunt of their own. First of all, a "witch hunt" implies a search for something that doesn't actually exist. Those who accused Cardinal Ratzinger of conducting a homosexual witch hunt to ferret out homosexual priests—which, of course, he has not done, were homosexual activists themselves. Calling Ratzinger a "homophobe," in 1998, the British gay lobbyist group Outrage! issued a statement seeking information about Ratzinger's sexual history. Presuming that everyone has a sordid sexual past— "skeletons in the closet"—Outrage! asked, "What do you know about his sexuality? Is there someone you know who might have inside knowledge? We need details that can be corroborated. Can you help? We do not know whether Ratzinger is gay: but, if he is, he deserves to be outed because he is arguably the most homophobic of all Vatican leaders, being responsible for two of the most virulently antigay declarations ever made by the Catholic leadership. . . . Help us expose this religious homophobe, who is damaging the lives of queers."[10]

Cardinal Ratzinger elicited such a strong reaction because he has consistently reiterated in strong, clear and direct language, the Church's opposition to the multi-faceted "gay agenda." The homosexualists are particularly put off by Ratzinger's characterization of homosexual acts as "intrinsically evil" and homosexual inclinations as "objectively disordered."[11] But their problem, whether they realize it or not, is not so much with Pope Benedict XVI as it is with the teachings of the Catholic Church. Proponents of the normalization of homosexuality in society are ultimately at war with Catholic truth. They want to be accommodated, and to be accommodated they want nothing short of a sea change in the Church's teaching on human sexuality, which is based on the natural law—not merely an opinion that fluctuates with the changing times, but an unchanging truth.

That wording—"intrinsically evil" and "objectively disordered"—was later incorporated into the *Catechism of the Catholic Church*, but it first appeared in the 1986 document "The Pastoral Care of Homosexual Persons," authored by

Cardinal Ratzinger and released as an official Vatican statement from the Congregation for the Doctrine of the Faith and approved by Pope John Paul II.[12] The full wording of the passage is: "Although the particular inclination of the homosexual person is not a sin, it is a more or less strong tendency ordered toward an intrinsic moral evil; and thus the inclination itself must be seen as an objective disorder."[13] These few words formed the basis for many of the struggles in the Church over the following two decades concerning the implications of the Church's teaching on homosexuality and ministry to homosexuals.

Days after the election of Pope Benedict, Matt Foreman, executive director of the National Gay and Lesbian Task Force, told the *San Francisco Chronicle* that he left the Catholic Church in 1986 precisely because of Cardinal Ratzinger's letter on the pastoral care of homosexuals, released that year. "It was so stunning in both the breadth and depth of condemnation," Foreman said of the pastoral letter. "The cardinals have elected the most outspoken and venomous opponent of equal rights for gay people in the Catholic Church's hierarchy."[14]

The letter warned of "deceitful propaganda" from pro-homosexual lobbyists, and instructed bishops not to accept groups that neglect or undermine the teaching of the Church. It also warned that civil legislation introduced to protect homosexual behavior will inevitably lead to "other distorted notions and practices" gaining ground in society—a prophetic statement, considering that through the course of 1990s the homosexual subculture became increasingly tolerated in western society, and is now protected and celebrated in many countries, even to the point of recognizing same-sex "marriages" and civil unions.

The letter was prophetic in a number of other ways as well. Cardinal Ratzinger recognized back in 1986 that homosexual activists had designs to use the Catholic Church, through her pastors, to promote the many aspects of the "gay agenda," starting with the acceptance of homosexuality by society and culminating in a reform of the sacred institution of marriage to include legally-sanctioned, if not Church-sanctioned, same-sex partnerships. Ratzinger identified the modus operandi of those within the Church seeking to achieve these ends. "There are many who seek to create confusion regarding the Church's position [on homosexuality] and then to use that confusion to their own advantage."[15] Cardinal Ratzinger went on to explain that various pressure groups attempt to give the impression that they represent all homosexual persons who are Catholic, when in fact the membership of these activist groups consist solely of those who either ignore authentic Church teaching or seek to undermine it. These groups bring together, "under the aegis of Catholicism, homosexual persons who have no intention of abandoning their homosexual behavior."[16]

Cardinal Ratzinger explained that one tactic used by homosexualists inside and outside the Church is to protest that any criticisms of or reservations about homosexuals, their activities, or their lifestyle, are simply forms of unjust discrimination—the invention of a "culture of homophobia." This became the subject of the second major document concerning homosexuality released from the CDF under Cardinal Ratzinger: the 1992 pastoral letter entitled, "Some Considerations Concerning the Catholic Response to Legislative Proposals on the Non-Discrimination of Homosexual Persons." As the title suggests, the letter was directed at the movement to include "homosexual orientation" as part of protected civil rights in various countries, including the United States. These initiatives, warned Cardinal Ratzinger, not only condone homosexual behavior and lifestyles, but will also have a negative impact on the family and society. "Such things as the adoption of children, the employment of teachers, the housing needs of genuine families, landlords' legitimate concerns in screening potential tenants, for example, are often implicated."[17] In response, the cardinal made clear that "sexual orientation" does not constitute a quality comparable to race, religion, or ethnicity when it comes to nondiscrimination. "Unlike these," he stated, "homosexual orientation is an objective disorder and evokes moral concern." The homosexual lobby twisted Cardinal Ratzinger's five-page statement to accuse him of denying "equal rights" to homosexuals. He was also denounced—again—as a "bigot," a "homophobe," and a "witch hunter."

More than a decade later, in the thick of the push for legalization of homosexual unions, same-sex marriage, and adoption by homosexual couples in many Western nations, Cardinal Ratzinger released the third and last of his pastoral letters concerning homosexual issues through the Congregation for the Doctrine of the Faith. Entitled "Considerations Regarding Proposals to Give Legal Recognition to Unions Between Homosexual Persons" and released in July 2003, it was interpreted by some as Cardinal Ratzinger's "battle plan" to guide Catholic politicians (and others) to oppose legalization of same-sex marriage and homosexual adoptions. "There are absolutely no grounds for considering homosexual unions to be in any way similar or even remotely analogous to God's plan for marriage and family," wrote the future Pope Benedict. "Marriage is holy, while homosexual acts go against the natural moral law."[18]

The first public pronouncement from the Vatican under Benedict XVI was a strongly worded condemnation of a bill in Spain that not only allows same-sex marriage in the once-Catholic stronghold of Europe; it also requires mayors of every Spanish city to perform these state-sanctioned ceremonies. The Vatican called the bill "iniquitous" and appealed to Catholics to resist the new law even if it meant they might lose their jobs.

—

Accusations of Ratzinger's "witch hunt" were made in reference to the cardinal's necessary censures handed out to priests and religious who were promoting teachings on homosexuality contrary to the faith. Many, doing so under the guise of "ministering to lesbians and gays," were actually condoning homosexual acts and encouraging same-sex partnerships. In other words, Cardinal Ratzinger first laid out the law, and then he set out to enforce that law, all in the name of the faithful's right to receive the authentic teachings of the Catholic Church.

John J. McNeill, a former Jesuit priest and author of *The Church and the Homosexual*, argued that homosexual relationships should be judged by the same moral criteria as heterosexual relationships. Among other claims contrary to the teachings of the Church, the Jesuit priest and psychotherapist contended that the Bible does not condemn homosexuality, including homosexual acts—an argument popularly taken up by many other Catholic theologians since that time in an effort to demonstrate the "meaninglessness" of Church teaching on sexuality. McNeill is also credited for first applying the principles of liberation theology (another erroneous theological current condemned by Cardinal Ratzinger) to homosexuality. He is the author of two volumes that lay out this thesis of what he calls "gay and lesbian liberation, self-acceptance and spiritual maturity": his 1988 book T*aking a Chance on God: Liberating Theology for Gays and Lesbians, Their Lovers, Friends and Families* and his 1995 book *Freedom, Glorious Freedom: The Spiritual Journey to the Fullness of Life for Gays, Lesbians and Everybody Else*.

McNeill, a co-founder of the New York City chapter of Dignity, had been censured by the Vatican for his writings on homosexuality since 1977, but continued his "ministry" in workshops, conferences, lectures, and in his personal psychotherapy practice. Cardinal Ratzinger realized that for McNeill, the mission of his priesthood had shifted from proclaiming the Gospel of Christ to disseminating homosexual propaganda. In 1986, the priest was instructed by the Congregation for the Doctrine of the Faith to cease his "ministry to gays and lesbians." McNeill subsequently left the Jesuits and later the priesthood rather than accept Cardinal Ratzinger's censure.

"I was doing a lot of work with AIDS in New York City and was ordered to give that up," McNeill told a New York audience in 2005, shortly after the election of Pope Benedict. "I could not give that up," he said, calling Ratzinger "the most vicious homophobe that [homosexuals] have had to deal with over the past 15 years. His letters on gay rights show no compassion or sense of God's love. They are purely political letters"[19]

McNeill's account of his "silencing" was incomplete at best. Cardinal Ratzinger has always acknowledged the appropriateness of assisting those who suffer from AIDS or any other disease. In fact, it is well known that Cardinal John J. O'Connor, another of McNeill's sworn enemies, regularly visited and comforted AIDS patients, mainly homosexual men, in a New York hospital.[20] Cardinal O'Connor talked of his own work with these patients as a charitable work of mercy and encouraged other Catholics to do likewise. McNeill's "work with AIDS" was of a very different nature. He was not as much concerned with comforting the sick as he was affirming the homosexual in his persistent sin. His life work, in fact, was demonizing the Church's teaching on human sexuality. He was lauded by the abortion lobby group Catholics for a Free Choice for saying, "If you must choose between the Church teachings being wrong, or God being a sadist, by all means, choose that the Church teachings are wrong."[21] After leaving the priesthood, McNeill continued to counsel homosexuals in his psychotherapy practice and remained persistent in his opposition to the teachings of the Church. In the preface to the fourth edition of his book *The Church and the Homosexual*, McNeill calls on the Vatican to make a "public act of repentance for its homophobia."

McNeill was the first in a line of censures over the homosexual issue that included high profiles cases such as Fr. Matthew Fox and Fr. Andrew Guindon. In 1996, Cardinal Ratzinger even effected the replacement of the head of the Society of St. Paul over the order's consistent advancement of the homosexual agenda in their flagship publication *Famiglia Christiana*, even after receiving several warnings from Vatican officials.

The most celebrated censure over homosexual "ministry" was that of Fr. Robert Nugent, a member of the Society of the Divine Savior (Salvatorians) and Sr. Jeannine Gramick, a School Sister of Notre Dame. In 1977 the pair founded New Ways Ministry near Washington, D.C. According to its literature, the organization claims to engage in "gay-positive ministry of advocacy and justice" in order to promote "reconciliation between lesbian and gay Catholics and the wider Catholic community." The group has sponsored workshops in a majority of U.S. dioceses, where Fr. Nugent and Sr. Gramick's influence has spread.

In 1999, Cardinal Ratzinger wrote in his decree of censure that from the beginning of their ministry, the priest and nun advanced "doctrinally unacceptable positions regarding the sinfulness of homosexual acts and the objective disorder of the homosexual inclination."[22] Although the media and Nugent and Gramick's supporters took the opportunity to vilify Ratzinger and Pope John Paul as homophobic reactionaries, the investigation of the pair's writings and teachings took nearly two decades, during which time they were both given several opportunities to clarify their positions and correct their errors. Both refused.

The controversy began in 1984 when Cardinal James Hickey, Archbishop of Washington, informed Nugent and Gramick that they could no longer pursue their activities in his archdiocese. Cardinal Hickey had given the pair several opportunities to clarify their positions and to justify their activities before censuring them locally. At the same time, the Vatican Congregation for Institutes of Consecrated Life ordered both of them to separate themselves from New Ways Ministry. They were also informed that they were not to undertake any ministry without faithfully presenting the Church's teaching regarding the "intrinsic evil" of homosexual acts.

Although Nugent and Gramick removed themselves from leadership positions at New Ways Ministry, they did not heed the Vatican order. They continued to be involved with activities organized by New Ways Ministry and persisted to promote ambiguous positions on homosexuality, presenting the teaching of the Church as one possible option among others and as open to change. They also explicitly criticized Cardinal Ratzinger's *Letter on the Pastoral Care of Homosexual Persons* and other magisterial documents pertaining to human sexuality. Because of their continued activities, the Vatican continued to receive complaints about them from U.S. bishops, asking for clarification of their status. As a result, in 1988 the Vatican formed a commission to evaluate their public statements and activities in order to determine whether these were faithful to Church teaching. The commission was headed by Detroit's Cardinal Adam Maida.

In 1992, Nugent and Gramick aided the Vatican commission in their investigation by assembling their activities and thinking on homosexuality in a widely disseminated book, *Building Bridges: Gay and Lesbian Reality and the Catholic Church*. Two years later, the Maida commission issued its findings, citing a number of serious errors. These included the following from *Building Bridges*:

- Various forms of sexual intercourse, including homosexual acts, might be morally acceptable since these acts are not necessarily "unnatural" (44).
- In specific cases the "general objective norm about the morality of homogenital acts" can be "qualified" or "even suspended" (p. 151).

- It is wrong for the Church to "punish lesbian and gay persons" when they are simply being "true to their natures" (187).
- The "homosexual orientation" itself is "morally neutral" and can be compared to being "left-handed" (60).
- If a homosexual relationship is stable and faithful, this fact can possibly justify homosexual acts within such a relationship (61-63).
- Cardinal Ratzinger's teaching, in his 1986 *Letter on the Pastoral Care of Homosexual Persons*, that the homosexual inclination is an "objective disorder" does not reflect the "real experience" of homosexual persons and needs to be rejected in order to assist gay and lesbian people to know that they are not "abnormal, sick, sinful, or criminal" (189).
- The 1986 Letter betrays "little pastoral concern" (72) and sets back for at least 20 years "outreach to lesbian and gay Catholics" (72, 119).[23]

Nugent and Gramick were invited to respond to the findings. When they did so, the commission forwarded its recommendation to the Vatican. The commission had found "serious deficiencies" in their writings and pastoral activities, which were "incompatible with the fullness of Christian morality." Since the problems with the pair's work were of a doctrinal nature, the case was forwarded to the Congregation for the Doctrine of the Faith in 1995.

Cardinal Ratzinger immediately gave them another opportunity to clarify their positions in light of the commission's findings. He expressed the hope that they would be willing to express their assent to Catholic teaching on homosexuality and to correct the identified errors in their writing. Their responses, dated February 22, 1996, were judged by Ratzinger's congregation as "not sufficiently clear to dispel the serious ambiguities of their position."[24] Cardinal Ratzinger said that the pair had demonstrated a clear understanding of the Church's authentic teaching on homosexuality, but were unwilling to profess their adherence to or belief in that teaching. Furthermore, Nugent and Gramick released a second book in 1995 entitled *Voices of Hope: A Collection of Positive Catholic Writings on Gay and Lesbian Issues*, published by the Center for Homophobia Education. The writings presented in this volume indicated that the two authors were still committed to disseminating the same ideas that were fundamentally opposed to Church teaching on human sexuality.

At that point Cardinal Ratzinger decided the Nugent-Gramick case should be solved according to the procedure outlined in the Congregation for the Doctrine of the Faith's "Regulations for Doctrinal Examination."[25] On October 8, 1997, the cardinals and bishops who make up the congregation judged the statements of the two authors to be "erroneous and dangerous." Nugent and Gramick were then given yet another chance to respond to the *contestatio*, their syllabus of errors, of which the following is a summary:

- Homosexual feelings and behaviors are described as "natural";
- The authors' activities and writings are directed toward the promotion of views of sexuality which transcend biological and physical differences;
- Experience becomes the criterion through which the objective norms of morality are judged and set aside (e.g., in *Building Bridges*, the authors recount that many Catholic gay and lesbian persons have prayed to God and have come to a "conscience decision" that their life experience, though contrary to the Church's teaching, does not separate them from God or the Church):
- The authors' use of documents fails to distinguish the relative authority of these texts;
- In *Voices of Hope*, the authors selectively edit magisterial documents in such a way as to consistently excise the Church's teaching on the immorality of homosexual acts;
- The authors appeal to the category of "experience" of lesbian and gay people becomes the criterion for criticisms of the teaching of the Magisterium;
- Erroneous propositions are presented as rhetorical questions which are left unanswered;
- The authors state that "we may have to choose between 'defending Church teaching' and proclaiming Jesus' message of love";

- In the authors' writings homosexuality is judged to be superior to heterosexuality;
- The dissemination of the authors' errors promotes the legal recognition of homosexual unions and thus constitutes also an attack against the divine institution of marriage;
- The authors reinterpret the word "celibacy" to mean something far different from what the Catholic Church has always intended.[26]

Nugent and Gramick responded in 1998, but the members of Cardinal Ratzinger's congregation unanimously agreed that neither response was adequate. Both had sought to justify the publication of their two books, and neither expressed assent to the Church's teaching on homosexuality.

Despite the obstinacy of Nugent and Gramick, the Congregation gave them both one last opportunity to formulate a public declaration of their acceptance of Church teaching and to acknowledge the syllabus of errors identified in their books. These declarations were examined in October 1998, and—again—were determined to be insufficient to resolve the problems associated with their pastoral ministry. Sr. Gramick, Cardinal Ratzinger wrote in his 1999 notification, "simply refused to express any assent whatsoever to the teaching of the Church on homosexuality. Father Nugent was more responsive, but not unequivocal in his statement of interior assent to the teaching of the Church."[27] He refused to state that homosexual acts are "intrinsically disordered," and he called into question the definitive and unchangeable nature of Catholic doctrine in this area.

Thus, after almost two decades of investigation and repeated attempts to allow the New Ways Ministry pair to correct their erroneous teachings, Cardinal Ratzinger issued the following notification on May 31, 1999:

> Father Nugent and Sister Gramick have often stated that they seek, in keeping with the Church's teaching, to treat homosexual persons "with respect compassion and sensitivity." However, the promotion of errors and ambiguities is not consistent with a Christian attitude of true respect and compassion: Persons who are struggling with homosexuality, no less than any others, have the right to receive the authentic teaching of the Church from those who minister to them.
>
> The ambiguities and errors of the approach of Father Nugent and Sister Gramick have caused confusion among the Catholic people and have harmed the community of the Church. For these reasons, Sister Jeannine Gramick, SSND, and Father Robert Nugent, SDS, are permanently prohibited from any pastoral work involving homosexual persons and are ineligible, for an undetermined period, for any office in their respective religious institutes.[28]

Once this notification was made public, the media came to the aid of the "homosexual ministry" pair and vilified Cardinal Ratzinger as a "Grand Inquisitor." The headline in the *San Francisco Examiner* read, "Vatican Nixes Catholic Gay Ministry." The *Washington Post* labeled the decision "a kind of public shaming," telling parishes across the nation that Gramick and Nugent "are anathema to the Church."[29]

It is difficult to imagine more judicious proceedings than those undertaken by Cardinal Ratzinger in the Nugent-Gramick affair, but that did not stop the supporters of New Ways–style homosexual ministry from using the case as a battering ram to vilify the future pope. Cardinal Ratzinger's critics, of course, were much less interested in the process than the outcome. His critics fundamentally do not believe that anyone who supports their pet causes ought to be disciplined in any way by anyone, least of all by an authority figure in the Vatican.

Fr. Nugent accepted the Vatican's ruling "as a son of the Church, a presbyter and a member of a religious congregation with a vow of obedience."[30] Sr. Gramick, however, did not. She continued to be a vocal critic of Church teaching and of Cardinal Ratzinger. Upon Benedict's election to the papacy, Gramick predicted that Ratzinger would "prevent the Church from moving into the 21st century and out of the Middle Ages. It does not bode well for people who are concerned for lesbian and gay people in the Church."[31]

— 7 —

Insisting Upon Sound Doctrine

The problem central to our time is the emptying of the historic figure of Jesus Christ. An impoverished Jesus cannot be the sole Savior and Mediator. . . . We must go back clearly to the Jesus of the Gospels, because he alone is the true historic Jesus.

Joseph Cardinal Ratzinger, 2001[1]

Of course, it was by no means only the subject of homosexuality that captured Cardinal Ratzinger's full attention at the Congregation for the Doctrine of the Faith. He spent twenty-four years contending with a long list of dubious teachings emanating from the mouths and pens of theologians. As the Vatican's "enforcer" on doctrinal issues, he was not shy about drawing a line in the sand and properly wielding the authority of his office in order to protect the deposit of faith from being corrupted by theologians, pastors, and even bishops. It was the future Pope Benedict, for example, who tackled liberation theology which was rapidly spreading throughout South and Central America, as well as parts of Asia and Africa, by the time he came to the Vatican in 1981. This widely popularized movement sought to use Marxist principals in order to address the problem of poverty in the Third World.

In 1984, Cardinal Ratzinger released an "Instruction on Certain Aspects of the Theology of Liberation." While applauding efforts to promote social justice, the cardinal criticized theologians who borrow "in an insufficiently critical manner" from Marxist ideology, reducing salvation to liberation of the poor from worldly oppressors rather than liberation from "radical sin." This theological deviation, he wrote, "tends inevitably to betray the cause of the poor" because, in practice, it leads the oppressed to accept a series of positions which are "incompatible with the Christian vision of humanity."[2] The result, he said, is too often violent class struggle and political amorality. In other words, it is impossible to invoke Marxist principles and terminology without ultimately embracing Marxist methods and goals.

The movement had been growing since the mid-1960s, exported from European universities under the influence of Socialism and Marxist theory to the poorest regions of the Third World. By the time Cardinal Ratzinger formally condemned liberation theology with his systematic analysis, the concept had almost become a household term, even though most people still had no real idea of what it meant. Many Catholics, the cardinal recognized, confused liberation theology with the Church's authentic teaching on the "preferential option for the poor." Uneducated and often intemperate critics accused Ratzinger and the Vatican of dismissing the cries of the poor. The cardinal's instruction, if carefully read, affirms the Church's commitment to condemn abuses, injustices, and attacks against freedom wherever they occur. But the Church will do so, he emphasized, with Christian principles, not Marxist ones. Raw political power can never be used as a substitute for God's will.

The 1984 instruction dealt with the subject in a clear and direct way, but without mentioning any names. It didn't take long, however, before Ratzinger's office addressed individual theologians who were proponents of this condemned theology. He called several of the more outspoken priest theologians to Rome and later, after long discussions and investigation, censured them for abandoning the Church's principles and mission in favor of promoting a radical political agenda that undermined both the Catholic Church and the poor, who they were supposed to be "liberating."

Fr. Gustavo Gutierrez of Peru, known as the father of liberation theology, was the first target of the inquiry. But Brazilian Leonardo Boff was considered the leading proponent of liberation theology. His talent for using the mass media to amplify his ideas certainly made him the most influential liberation theologian. Boff, a Franciscan priest and one of Cardinal Ratzinger's former theology students in Germany, was accompanied to Rome by two archbishops to help him defend his ideas: Cardinals Evaristo Arns from Sao Paolo and Aloiso Lorscheider from Fortalezza, both of whom strongly supported the Brazilian theologian. Nevertheless, Boff was censured in 1985 by the Congregation for the Doctrine of the Faith and his books were banned for use in Catholic seminaries and universities, where they had been used for years as a popular theology textbooks. Boff left the priesthood in 1992 and, because of Cardinal Ratzinger's internal inquiry, the movement gradually faded—at least in its original form. The same principles would later be applied in different ways, to new groups claiming to be oppressed by society—by radical feminists, ecologists, AIDS "victims," and homosexual activists, for example.

—

While Cardinal Ratzinger believed that liberation theology in its more radical forms was the most urgent challenge facing the Church during the 1980s, in the following decade—and up to the present time—the cardinal publicly recognized "relativism" as having become the central problem of the faith. The basis of this philosophy is that no one, not even the Church, can presume to know the true way. Pontius Pilate summed it up nicely when he said: "What is truth?" Relativism in theology therefore became Cardinal Ratzinger's particular concern.

One manifestation of theological relativism he addressed publicly was the "theology of religious pluralism." During the

1990s, the cardinal spearheaded a Vatican campaign against this theology which called into question the very essence of the Catholic faith: that Jesus Christ is the only Son of God and that through Him, and only through Him, comes salvation. The pluralist theology of world religions, which has been developing progressively since the 1950s in the Catholic Church, affirms that there is no binding and valid truth in the figure of Jesus Christ. The faith of the Church therefore is reduced to "fundamentalism," which is seen as the leading threat against the supreme good of tolerance and freedom. In a 1996 speech to the presidents of the doctrinal commissions of the Latin American bishops' conferences, Cardinal Ratzinger called this a new form of the Marxist conception of the world. Religious relativism, a "typical product of the Western world," is all the more insidious in that "it puts itself in contact with the philosophical and religious intuitions of Asia, particularly those of the Indian subcontinent."[3] Eastern religions present a problem to Western Christianity precisely because they have a natural affinity for secular relativism.

In his watershed 1996 talk in Mexico, Cardinal Ratzinger singled out American theologian and ex-priest Paul Knitter. For Knitter and other religious pluralists, Christianity does not have a right to make an exclusive claim to the truth. Nor is Jesus understood as the Christ, but rather just one of many historical incarnations of the Savior Son.

The kind of religious pluralism promoted by Knitter has a number of ramifications that may not be immediately apparent. A quick review of what the theologian considers his "dialogical odyssey" reveals why Cardinal Ratzinger used him as an example of what he condemns as a theology of "methodological doubt."

In an introduction to Knitter's 1995 book, *One Earth Many Religions: Multifaith Dialogue & Global Responsibility*, dissident Swiss theologian Hans Küng wrote, "I have always maintained that a Christian theologian, even in dialogue with followers of other religions, must defend the normativity and finality of Jesus Christ as God's revelatory event for Christians."[4] Knitter, however, according to Küng, goes a bit further, crossing a theological "rubicon" wherein he places Jesus alongside just about any other historical figure who has been considered a prophet in the religious sense. In other words, Knitter dismisses the binding and unique valid truth found in the figure of Jesus Christ.

Knitter, who considers himself to be evolving "dialogically," speaks of himself and his "dialogical odyssey" quite self-consciously throughout his numerous published works. Like the architect who designs a monument to himself, Knitter has spent a career designing a man-made theology that fits his ever-evolving theological outlook. In *One Earth Many Religions,* Knitter explains that odyssey in a nutshell. He writes that he was attracted to join the Divine Word Missionaries (the "SVDs" or Societas Verbi Divini) in 1958 because of his sincere desire to convert the world to the Catholic faith. "Five times a day, in our seminary prayers," wrote Knitter, "we stormed heaven with the invocation: 'May the darkness of sin and the night of heathenism vanish before the light of the Word and the Spirit of grace.'"[5]

Knitter explained that he wished to travel to distant lands to make converts of such "heathens." But once in the SVD seminary he was the one who was "enlightened and converted." During those years SVD missionaries returning home on furlough, he said, would often stop at the seminary to give presentations to the future missionaries about the missions in distant lands. "In their slide lectures," he wrote, "in their colorful, often moving stories of encounters with Hindus, Buddhists, [and] primal religious believers, I gradually realized that the SVDs were not really practicing or experiencing what they were praying about." Knitter noted that the missionaries talked more about the beauty of Hinduism or Buddhism than about "their pervasive and perverse darkness of sin."

In 1965 while taking courses at Rome's Gregorianum, Knitter became enraptured with Jesuit theologian Karl Rahner. "Rahner's theologically honed case that Christians not only can but must look upon other religions as 'legitimate' and as 'ways of salvation' was a breath of fresh, liberating air for me. It enabled me to make sense of what I had been seeing in the religious world beyond Christianity and to shake free of what I felt was the undergrounded hubris of Christian claims to be the only authentic religion."[6]

Once ordained a priest of the SVDs, Knitter moved on to study at the University of Marburg's Department of Protestant Theology, founded under "the Reformers." There he wrote a dissertation entitled "Toward a Protestant Theology of Religions," in which he criticized Protestant theologians for not going far enough in their recognition of salvation in religions outside of Christianity. Knitter admits, however, that at the time he was writing his doctorate, he was still "limited" by his belief in Rahner's "anonymous Christ" working in other religions (that is, non-Christians are saved by Christ working anonymously within their own religions).

"I myself," wrote Knitter, "was not able to imagine that such wisdom and grace in other traditions could be anything else but 'reflections' of the fullness of truth and grace incarnated in Jesus the Christ."[7] His doctoratal work was, however, the first step towards Knitter's full liberation from the Catholic Church's understanding of the Gospel.

After teaching for several years at the Catholic Theological Union in Chicago, Knitter left the priesthood in 1975 and began teaching theology courses on Hinduism and Buddhism at Xavier University in Cincinnati. Looking to his role models, Thomas Merton and Raimon Panikkar, Knitter wrote that he returned, after years of neglect, to daily meditation. But he gave up his "pre-Vatican II" practice of Christian mental prayer in favor of Eastern zazen meditation (sometimes known as "centering prayer"), which, he claims, was instrumental in making him self-aware of his own evolving theology of religious pluralism.

In 1985 Orbis Books (the Maryknoll Society) published his survey of Christian attitudes toward world religions, another self-conscious attempt to understand his own evolving dialogical journey. In his preface of that book, *No Other Name?*, Knitter candidly admits that his motivation to write the book arose out of his need to integrate what he had learned from other religious traditions into his own. Knitter concludes by proposing a new "more authentic" Christology rooted in the explicitly modernist concept of doctrinal evolution.[8] Knitter contends that the true professional Christian theologian must subscribe to a "global or inter-religious theology" which recognizes "a kind of Teilhardian religious evolution."[9] In other words, all religious truth, according to Knitter, is relative, is in constant flux, and is evolving through time. He further argues for a conversion from "Christocentricity" to a vague "theocentricity."

In 1987, Knitter continued to explore his theological idiosyncrasies by editing, along with Protestant scholar John Hick, *The Myth of Christian Uniqueness: Toward a Pluralistic Theology of Religions*, a book addressed directly by Cardinal Ratzinger in his 1996 talk in Mexico City. Knitter's own contribution to that volume was entitled, "Toward a Liberation Theology of Religions."[10] This article drew upon his experiences with the Sanctuary Movement—"a loose ecumenical bonding of churches and synagogues who," as Knitter describes, "were publicly providing shelter and support to Central American refugees fleeing the poverty and dangers of U.S.-sponsored wars in their countries."[11] After collaborating with Jesuit Jon Sobrino and Lutheran Bishop

Medardo Gomez in El Salvador, "liberation theology," writes Knitter, "became for me not just a 'new method' but a matter of making sense of religion and of being a faithful disciple of Jesus."[12]

In the early 1980s, says Knitter, after reflecting on religious encounters with Native Americans, he began to apply his liberation theology to all "earthlings"—plant, animal, earth and human—developing his theory of eco-human justice and well-being. "Just as human suffering and ecological suffering have common causes," wrote Knitter, "they will have common solutions. To speak of justice and liberation, therefore, one must intend eco-human justice and liberation."[13] Thus, Knitter evolved into a theologian promoting what he calls "global responsibility."

In 1995, he published *One Earth Many Religions*, tying together his two main developed theological concepts of "multifaith dialogue" and "global responsibility." In this book, writes Knitter, "I want to clarify the journey I have been on . . . and I want to do so in conversation with others who are also searching for truth and values. I hope to lay the foundation—and maybe the first few floors—of a theology of religions that will be liberative, that is, a theology that will grow out of and contribute to the salvation and well-being of suffering humanity and Earth; and of a theology of liberation that will be dialogical, that is, a theology that is able to embrace and learn from the potential of many religions for promoting human and planetary life."[14]

But he wishes to redefine the terms "liberation"—so as not to be limited to the association with Marxist economic theory and "pluralism"—because pluralist theologians "want to pile all religions on a happy syncretist bandwagon." Nevertheless, the latest incarnation of Knitter's theology, the so-called "global responsibility," includes liberation theology in the Marxist economic sense, but is also applied to eco-human justice and well-being, with the ultimate intent to "resolve the human and ecological suffering prevalent throughout the world."[15]

Knitter also co-authored *Faith, Religion, and Theology: A Contemporary Introduction*, intended to be the primary textbook in basic courses on the Catholic faith for freshman at Catholic colleges and to introduce them to a mature view of their Catholic faith that goes beyond the catechetical instruction they received in CCD. In the section authored by Knitter, he projects his affinity for Buddhism by equating it with Christianity. Although there are a number of references to the Buddhist concept of "nirvana" in the book's index, there are none for heaven, paradise, the beatific vision, hell, or purgatory. In fact there are numerous references in the index to obscure Buddhist and Hindu terms like Bodhisattva, tanha, sangha, dukkha, darshana, anicca, ahimsa, avatar, anatta, and avidya, while important Christian terms like Mary, Mass, sacrifice, saint, apostle, repentance, incarnation, confirmation, marriage, anointing, penance, and ordination are conspicuously absent.[16]

Knitter's fascination with Buddhism led him to include an appendix to the section on religion entitled: "Jesus and Buddha: A Conversation." This is an imaginary conversation between Jesus and Siddartha Gautama Buddha on various religious matters. This could have been done cleverly by juxtaposing the words of Jesus from the New Testament with those of the Buddha from Buddhist sources. Instead Knitter gives his own thoughts on what Jesus and Buddha would say. The conversation, therefore, serves as a forum for Knitter to put his own views into Christ's mouth. Knitter does not present Catholicism as the one true faith. Rather , he takes an indifferent attitude toward religions generally as sociological, anthropological, and psychological phenomena among human beings in which one system of belief is as good as another and "true beliefs" are unnecessary as long as everyone is "sincere."

Although Knitter was singled out by Cardinal Ratzinger in his 1996 speech, the lay theologian was never formally censured nor were his books condemned, most likely because Knitter was a laicized priest—consequently, the Vatican had no direct control over his teachings as a Catholic theologian—and none of his books carried an imprimatur, a sign of approbation by his local bishop that his books contained no theological errors. Thus, the cardinal conducted his investigations elsewhere.

In October 1998, for example, Ratzinger began to investigate the writings of Fr. Jacques Dupuis, a prominent

Belgian Jesuit theologian teaching in the heart of Rome at the Gregorian University, arguably the most authoritative of the pontifical universities, one that for centuries has educated the leaders of the Catholic Church worldwide. Many bishops, cardinals, and popes can be counted among its alumni. Fr. Dupuis also served as an advisor to the Pontifical Council for Interreligious Dialogue and even helped draft the Vatican's 1991 guidelines on interreligious dialogue.

A few years later, upon the publication of his 1997 book *Toward a Christian Theology of Religious Pluralism*, Fr. Dupuis' prestigious post made him the most visible exponent of this "pluralistic theology of religions."[17] The book, used as the primary text for his courses, was endorsed with great praise by the Gregorian. A few months later, however, a scathing review published in *L'Avvenire* (April 14, 1998), the official newspaper of the Italian Bishops Conference, caught the attention of Cardinal Ratzinger. A two-year long investigation ensued.

In 1999, while under investigation by the Congregation for the Doctrine of the Faith, Fr. Dupuis was ordered to cease teaching at the Gregorian because his book was the primary text for his course. The notification of his censure by Cardinal Ratzinger came two years later. It stated that his book contained "ambiguities and difficulties on important points which could lead a reader to erroneous or harmful opinions."[18] Fr. Dupuis was criticized above all for giving the impression that Jesus was not the unique Savior of mankind, and that Eastern religions also provide a legitimate path to salvation, even apart from Christ.

Fr. Dupuis promoted an egalitarian form of interreligious dialogue that, as with Knitter, drew its inspiration from his personal experiences in Asia. "I went through a conversion by living for so many years in India. If I had not lived in India for 36 years," he said, "I would not preach the theology which I am preaching today. I consider my exposure to Hindu reality as the greatest grace I have received from God in my vocation as a theologian."[19] This "grace" is what permeates the writings of Jacques Dupuis. His emphasis as a theologian engaged in interreligious dialogue eschews Christian evangelization and converting unbelievers as St. Francis Xavier and other Jesuits had done in India in centuries past. Instead Fr. Dupuis focused on the search for divine revelation present in the Eastern religions.

Eastern mysticism has played no little part in the theology of religious pluralism. The censures handed down by Ratzinger's office provide a sort of Who's Who of Oriental Unbelief. In 1997, Sri Lanken Fr. Tissa Balasuriya became the first—and only—theologian to be formally excommunicated after an investigation by Cardinal Ratzinger. The Oblate priest came under fire for his controversial book entitled *Mary and Human Liberation* (1990). The book and its author were condemned for assailing essential articles of the Catholic creed—for example, Fr. Balasuriya casts doubt on the divinity of Christ and misrepresents the doctrine of original sin.[20] He was later reconciled with the Church after he—reluctantly—recanted his book and its teachings, vowing to assent to the Magisterial teachings of the faith. He has since been adopted by reformist Catholics, who look to him as something of a demigod, believing him to have all the qualities of the perfect reformed theologian.

The censure of Indian Jesuit Fr. Anthony DeMello, however, fully reflected Cardinal Ratzinger's deep misgivings about the impact of Eastern spirituality on Christian theology and the practice of the Catholic faith. DeMello's work was criticized by the Congregation for the Doctrine of the Faith for "relativizing" the faith and promoting "religious indifferentism."[21] Specifically, he was accused of having dissolved God, Jesus, and the Church into a cosmic, New Age spirituality more akin to the notions of Eastern mysticism. This censure, in particular, was significant and resonant, especially in the United States, because of DeMello's tremendous following. Eight of his books were published by Doubleday, the largest publishing company in the United States, and the combined sales of his books ran into the millions. Cardinal Ratzinger's letter to the bishops conferences around the world urged the Church's shepherds to have his books withdrawn where possible (in the case of Catholic publishers), or to ensure the books are printed with a notice indicating Fr. DeMello's teachings are contrary to the Catholic faith and may cause "grave harm." DeMello's case was unique in that his condemnation came ten years after his death.

In 2002, two more priest theologians were censured for their eastern-influenced teachings. Fr. Willigis Jäger, O.S.B. was ordered to cease all public activities, including lectures, courses and publications. The German Benedictine was faulted for downplaying the Christian concept of God as a person in his work as a "spiritual guide," and for stressing mystical experience above doctrinal truths. So deeply immersed in Eastern ideology was Jäger, he presented himself as a Zen Master and took the Zen name of Ko-un Roshi.[22]

In the same year, Fr. Joseph Imbach, a Conventual Franciscan, was suspended from his teaching duties at Rome's Bonaventura Faculty of Theology and assigned a year of "reflection." Fr. Imbach's writings had been under review by Cardinal Ratzinger's office for several years. Through the investigation, Ratzinger concluded that, based on the priest's writings, Imbach did not believe in the divinity of Jesus, that he rejected the magisterium of the Church, that he reduced the Gospels to "teaching texts" rather than historically reliable accounts, and that he excluded the possibility of miracles.[23] This theological dossier that reflects the general thinking of the so-called "Jesus Seminar" theologians. The Jesus Seminar is a Berkeley, California–based group of liberal New Testament scholars—Catholic and Protestant—dedicated to discerning a non-Christian Jesus hidden inside the Gospels.

The Seminar meets twice a year to dissect scriptural passages. Their goal is to separate historical fact from the fiction of the Bible. At each meeting, the Seminar debates technical papers submitted by the scholars. At the close of debate on each agenda item, Seminar participants vote by dropping colored beads into a box to indicate the degree of authenticity of Jesus' words or deeds. A red bead indicates Jesus undoubtedly said or did something very much like this; pink indicates that Jesus probably or might have said or did something like this; gray means Jesus probably did not do or say this; and black indicates that Jesus did not do or say this, but that it was concocted by men at a much later date.

Thus far the Jesus Seminar theologians have rejected as myth the resurrection of Jesus from the dead, the Virgin birth, all Gospel miracles, and more than 82 percent of the teachings traditionally attributed to Jesus. All are dismissed as legends with no historical foundation. Even the Lord's Prayer does not go untouched. In fact, the Seminar accepts only two words as authentic: "Our Father."

The complete results of the Jesus Seminar deliberations on the "sayings" of Jesus were published in 1993 as *The Five Gospels: The Search for the Authentic Words of Jesus.*[24] Out of the 1500 items reviewed, the Seminar concluded that only 18 percent were of probable authenticity. Likewise, in 1996 the Seminar published more of their findings in *The Acts of Jesus*. Out of 387 reports of 176 events, only ten were given the red rating.

In 2001, addressing the Tenth Synod of Bishops, Cardinal Ratzinger summed up the problem of the Seminar-style "historical Jesus" this way: "The problem central to our time is the emptying of the historic figure of Jesus Christ. An impoverished Jesus cannot be the sole Savior and Mediator, the God-with-us; thus, Jesus is substituted with the idea of the 'values of the kingdom,' and becomes a vain hope. We must go back clearly to the Jesus of the Gospels, because he alone is the true historic Jesus."[25]

—

The very public protest over Cardinal Ratzinger's censures precipitated the 1997 document *Ad Tuendam Fidem* released by the Congregation for the Doctrine of the Faith and signed by Cardinal Ratzinger. *Ad Tuendam Fidem* issued new norms aimed at safeguarding the rights of theologians accused of unorthodox teachings. It also tightened up the disciplinary provisions of canon law that deal with theological dissent. The four-page document added a new paragraph to the Code of Canon Law to defend the integrity of the faith against theological dissent. Pope John Paul II explained that the new paragraph makes clear the "serious obligation" of theologians to convey the faith accurately, and sets forth the canonical sanctions that may be imposed on those who fail to uphold this duty. Pope John Paul also reminded local bishops of their own obligation to see to it that the faith is upheld by the official teachers of the faith in their dioceses—those who teach at Catholic seminaries, colleges, and universities; and if such a person does not uphold the faith, the bishop is to apply a "just penalty."

The official commentary released alongside Pope John Paul's document was made by the Congregation for the

Doctrine of the Faith. Cardinal Ratzinger explained that there are two higher "categories" of Catholic truth. Category one, the "infallible," includes the Resurrection of Jesus, the Assumption of Mary, the sacrificial nature of the Mass, and the Immaculate Conception. Teachings from the second category, the "defined," includes papal infallibility, the evil of fornication and prostitution, the evil of euthanasia, and the impossibility of the ordination of women.

Cardinal Ratzinger's commentary also stated that persons who obstinately and persistently oppose a truth in the first category are "heretics." Those who oppose one of the truths in the second category are said not to be in full communion with the Church. Even a cursory examination of the many theologians who call themselves Catholic reveals that a significant number of them fall within one or another of these categories.

—

The 1990s was also the decade that saw the great push for the ordination of women to the priesthood in the Catholic Church. Radical feminists in several Western nations, most prominently in the U.S., Austria, and Switzerland, banned together with singular purpose: to fight for a women's "right" to holy orders. In May 1994, Pope John Paul released *Ordinatio Sacerdotalis*, which reaffirmed that the Church "has no authority whatsoever to confer priestly ordination on women and that this judgment is to be definitively held by all the

Church's faithful." This simple statement was supposed to put the matter to rest forever. Radical feminists, supported by progressive theologians throughout the world, did not accept the pope's teaching. A year later, in October 1995, the Congregation for the Doctrine of the Faith followed up with a "Reply ad Dubium." Addressed to the bishops throughout the world, Cardinal Ratzinger clarified that the teaching set forth by John Paul in *Ordinatio Sacerdotalis* was a teaching of the ordinary magisterium, and therefore had been "set forth infallibly." Ratzinger left no room for doubt, no room for compromise, and no room for dialogue. His response was clear and direct. In the eyes of the radical feminists, this document elevated Cardinal Ratzinger to Public Enemy Number Two, a close second to John Paul.

It is not surprising them that feminist leaders had harsh words in response to the election of Benedict XVI. Sister Maureen Fiedler of the liberal We Are Church movement told the *Hindustan Times* that when she heard the *Habemus Papam* from Cardinal Medina Estevez her heart sank. "One of the major changes I would have hoped for in a new pope was an openness to women," said Fiedler, a member of the Sisters of Loretto. "He simply has no record that would suggest that he's open . . . to more than 50 per cent of the Catholic community, to more than 50 per cent of the world," she added in rather simplistic language.[26] Another leading women's activist in the Church, Benedictine Sister Joan Chittister, agreed. She charged that Ratzinger had a "limited" understanding of women's issues, a thinly-veiled way of saying the new pope doesn't agree with her.[27] Joy Barnes of the Women's Ordination Conference said "Cardinal Ratzinger is a divisive person in the Church when we really needed someone to heal the Church."[28] Of course, Barnes believes that the Church can only be "healed" by a Pope who will ordain women.

— 8 —

Remodeling the Face of the Church

I am convinced that the ecclesial crisis in which we find ourselves today depends in great part upon the collapse of the liturgy, which at times is actually being conceived of etsi Deus non daretur: as though in the liturgy it did not matter any more whether God exists or whether He speaks to us and listens to us.

Joseph Cardinal Ratzinger, 1997[1]

In 1980, a year before John Paul appointed Cardinal Ratzinger to head the Congregation for the Doctrine of the Faith, the pope asked him to head the Congregation for Catholic Education. The cardinal declined, saying he felt shouldn't leave his post as Archbishop of Munich too soon. As a former university professor, Pope Benedict has a deep and abiding interest in Catholic education and seminary formation. Since his work at the Congregation for the Doctrine of the Faith was often closely linked to Catholic education (he was also a cardinal member of the Congregation for Catholic Education) during his twenty-four years at the Vatican he came to understand rather well the major problems facing Catholic education in many parts of the world: inadequate catechesis, sex education that undermines the teachings of the Church, as well as the "methodological doubt" that characterizes the teaching of many theologians, both in Catholic colleges and in seminaries. One of his most serious concerns, however, is that of the fundamental identity of Catholic educational institutions. The problem is that many of these institutions are Catholic in name only.

The new pope has given indications in his past writings and interviews that he might not be readily committed to expending Church resources in order to preserve institutions that are already lost to secularism. In his memoirs, Cardinal Ratzinger recalled the Church's struggle in Germany to keep possession of its schools under the Nazi regime: "It dawned on me that, with their insistence on preserving institutions, [the bishops] in part misread the reality. Merely to guarantee institutions is useless if there are no people to support those institutions from inner conviction."[2] Such is precisely the problem today in many countries. Institutions of Catholic education are often peopled by those whose ideas actually run counter to the mission of the Catholic Church. In fact, many Catholic colleges and universities have simply adopted the routine and educational mission of public institutions.

The most important document regarding Catholic education released during the John Paul pontificate was *Ex Corde Ecclesiae*—"from the heart of the Church." This document, promulgated on August 15, 1990, defines with papal authority what constitutes a university's entitlement to be called "Catholic." It was the fruit of many years of consultation carried on between the Vatican and Catholic university officials around the world. It states that professors of theology are required to overtly profess their allegiance to the Church's Magisterium as a key element in their being commissioned by the local bishop to carry on their teaching as Catholic theologians.

Ex Corde Ecclesiae unambiguously insists that this commissioning of theology professors, known as the *mandatum*, be a cornerstone and pledge of a Catholic university's identification with the Church. The document also emphasizes, reiterating the norms of canon law, that the local bishop is pastorally responsible for overseeing the university's teaching of the faith in the discipline of theology. In other words, the bishop is responsible for safeguarding the university's Catholic identity. Unfortunately, this canonical requirement has been deftly side-stepped since Vatican II and continues to be postponed by the bishops even now, more than a decade after the promulgation of *Ex Corde Ecclesiae*.

On a 1999 visit to a conference in Menlo Park, California, Cardinal Ratzinger addressed the hot topic of *Ex Corde Ecclesiae*'s *mandatum*. He said that by insisting on adherence to magisterial teaching, Rome actually promotes academic freedom. "As you see with a medical faculty, you have complete academic freedom, but the discipline is such that the obligation of what medicine is determines the exercise of this freedom. As a medical person, you cannot do what you will. You are in the service of life," Ratzinger said.[3] "So theology also has its inner exigencies. Catholic theology is not individual reflection but thinking with the faith of the church. If you will do other things and have other ideas of what God could be or could not be, there is the freedom of the person to do it, clearly. But one should not say this is Catholic theology."[4]

—

Another aspect of Catholic identity that is close to the heart of the new pope is that of the liturgy, which Cardinal Ratzinger believes is also too often Catholic in name only. In addition to penning the introduction to Msgr. Klaus Gamber's important book *The Reform of the Roman Liturgy*, in which he refers to the author as "the one scholar, who, among the army of pseudo-liturgists, truly represents the liturgical thinking of the center of the Church,"[5] Ratzinger has devoted two of his own books to the subject of Catholic liturgy, and has addressed the subject at length in at least two others. *A New Song for the Lord*, a collection of essays published between 1975 and 1995, is primarily a critique of the novelties introduced into the sacred rites following the Second Vatican Council (1962-65). He makes a convincing argument that these innovations are not only deviant with respect to liturgical norms, but have also had a negative influence upon the content and practice of the faith.

The cardinal's 1997 autobiography *Milestones: Memoirs 1927-1977* included his first sustained lament over the state of contemporary liturgy. He bluntly, though eloquently, blames the overall "crisis" in the Church on the collapse of the liturgy: "I am convinced that the ecclesial crisis in which we find ourselves today depends in great part upon the collapse of the liturgy, which at times is actually being conceived of *etsi Deus non daretur*: as though in the liturgy it did not matter any more whether God exists and whether He speaks to us and listens to us. But if in the liturgy the communion of faith no longer appears, nor the universal unity of the Church and her history, nor the mystery of the living Christ, where is it that the Church still appears in her spiritual substance?"[6]

Cardinal Ratzinger traces much of his criticism of contemporary liturgy back to the unprecedented manner in which Pope Paul VI "created" a new liturgical rite to replace the old rite. "I was dismayed by the banning of the old Missal," he wrote, "seeing that a similar thing had never happened in the entire history of the liturgy."[7] The future Pope Benedict called this "a break in the history of liturgy whose consequences could be tragic." Cardinal Ratzinger has long seen this "break" or "rupture" as vital to understanding the contemporary problems of liturgy. The way worship was presented in the years following was "as a workshop in which people are always busy at something."[8] The revolutionary way in which the old Mass was replaced by the new has created the impression that liturgy is something each community creates on its own rather than something which is "given." In the final analysis, each "community" wants to give itself its own liturgy. "But," he writes, "when the liturgy is something each one makes by himself, then it no longer gives us what is its true quality: encounter with the mystery which is not our product but our origin and the wellspring of our life."[9]

Although the Mass had undergone evolutionary changes throughout the history of the Church, it always did so organically. There was always a sense of "continuity" up until the eve of the Second Vatican Council, he wrote. In response to contemporary liturgical problems Cardinal Ratzinger has long advocated "a liturgical reconciliation, which goes back to recognizing the unity in the history of liturgy and understands Vatican II not as a break, but as a developing moment."[10] He states firmly in various venues that the sort of "liturgical renewal" that was hoped for when Pope John XXIII announced the ecumenical council is a far cry to what has happened since the promulgation of the New Mass in 1969. "Anyone like myself," he has written, "can only stand, deeply sorrowing, before the ruins of the very things they were concerned for."[11] He has also pointed out the contrast between the actual words of Vatican II's document on the liturgy and the practical application which followed in the four decades since then. *Sacrosanctum Concilium*, the Council's Constitution on the Sacred Liturgy, for example, recommended that Gregorian chant and Latin be given pride of place at Mass—a recommendation that has been heeded in far too few places.

His most definitive treatment on the subject of the liturgy, in which he outlines what he calls "the reform of the reform," comes by way of his 1999 book *Spirit of the Liturgy*, an homage to Fr. Romano Guardini's 1918 volume of the same name. From the very beginning of the "reform" Cardinal Ratzinger saw and denounced its distortions as a "fabrication" of the liturgy by "experts," even referring to modern liturgists as "the dead burying the dead."[12]

A primary target of the new pope's critique is Mass *versus populum*, to which he devotes an entire chapter in *Spirit of the Liturgy*. Mass "facing the people," he says, is an unwarranted innovation that has turned priests into entertainers: "We have to see [the priest], to respond to him, to know what he is doing. . . . Not surprisingly, people try to reduce this newly created role of assigning all kinds of liturgical functions to different individuals and entrusting the 'creative' planning of the liturgy to groups of people. . . to 'make their own contribution.' Less and less is God in the picture." He reiterated that sentiment in his Good Friday meditations just a month before his election to the papacy, when he addressed the abuse of the Sacrament of the Holy Eucharist. "We celebrate only ourselves," he said, instead of celebrating Christ.[13]

One of the main themes running through *Spirit of the Liturgy* is his critique of this "creativity," which he says often requires "directors of genius and talented actors."[14] He calls these self-appointed experts (who criticize, for example, the development of the tabernacle on the altar) "antiquarians," a term used by Pope Pius XII to refer to those who desire to return to some point in the distant past in order to resurrect some ancient form of liturgy, with total disregard to the centuries of organic liturgical development since then. Some liturgists are inclined to "archeological enthusiasm," Ratzinger observed in a review of Dom Alcuin Reid's *The Organic Development of Liturgy*.[15] They are trying to unearth the oldest form of the Roman liturgy in its original purity and attempting to cleanse it of all later additions, all in the name of renewal. Cardinal Ratzinger summarily dismissed this mentality, reminding liturgical enthusiasts that "liturgical reform is something different from archeological excavation."[16]

Ratzinger has also been concerned with the ever-growing trend toward conducting the liturgy as entertainment. For example, he excoriates the use of popular forms of music, such as rock, during the liturgy: "'Rock' . . . is the expression of elemental passions, and at rock festivals it assumes a cultic character, a form of worship, in fact, in opposition to Christian worship. People are, so to speak, released from themselves by the experience of being part of crowd and by the emotional shock of rhythm, noise, and special effects. However, in the ecstasy of having all their defenses torn down, the participants sink, as it were, beneath the elemental force of the universe."[17]

From his critique of "rock" he reasons that trying to attract young people to Mass by the use of "rock music" in the liturgy is pure folly and, in the final assessment, counterproductive, alienating them from true worship. With respect to pop music, and the kind of liturgical gesturing and dancing that often accompanies this approach to liturgy, Cardinal Ratzinger warns against the tendency to turn liturgy into a form of entertainment. "Whenever applause breaks out in the liturgy because of some human achievement, it is a sure sign that the essence of the liturgy has totally disappeared and been replaced by a kind of religious entertainment. Such attraction fades quickly—it cannot compete in the market of leisure pursuits, incorporating as it increasingly does various forms of religious titillation."[18]

With respect to this kind of liturgical showmanship, Cardinal Ratzinger never hid his reservations about the manner in which Pope John Paul II celebrated Mass throughout the world, especially during the annual World Youth Day celebrations. During John Paul's 2004 visit to Bern, Switzerland, for example, the celebration of the Youth Day Mass was likened to Woodstock, replete with screaming teens, MTV-style pop music, drum rhythms, and a swing Jazz performance. John L. Allen, the Rome correspondent for the *National Catholic Reporter*, asked a rhetorical question that might well have been on the mind of Cardinal Ratzinger: "Can a robust Catholic identity be forged by mimicking the modes of expression of the larger culture? Or would the Church do better to foster its own distinctive speech, prayer and devotions?"[19]

The papal liturgies of Pope Benedict XVI will be a study in contrast even if only judging from the earliest weeks of the Ratzinger papacy. As journalists struggled in the days following the election to divine the agenda of the new pontiff, the man who was Ratzinger gave only one clear indication. Speaking to the cardinals who had handed him the keys of St. Peter, Benedict made it clear that, above all else, the primary focus of his papacy would be the Holy Eucharist. Clearly, for the new pope, the form and substance of the Holy Sacrifice of the Mass are intimately connected.

The Mass of inauguration on Benedict's first Sunday as Supreme Pontiff was the earliest realization of this first point in the papal agenda. Solemnity without showmanship was the order of the day. A few days before the inauguration, the new pope told his master of ceremonies that he wanted to hold the Mass inside St. Peter's Basilica "because there the architecture better directs the attention toward Christ, instead of the Pope."[20] Nearly all the public papal Masses of the previous pontificate were held in St. Peter's Square outside in a space that is neither sacred nor even designed for celebration of the Mass. Only the large number of the faithful, which included one hundred thousand German pilgrims, induced him to change his mind and hold his first papal Mass outdoors.

Nevertheless, the ceremony began inside at the tomb of St. Peter beneath the high altar, where the pope received his pallium and fisherman's ring, the outward symbols of papal authority. From there, the pope and the cardinals processed through the nave of the basilica to the chanting of the *Laudes Regiae*. In fact, the Sistine Choir sang Gregorian chant and classic polyphony in Latin throughout the entire ceremony.

Pope Benedict is also a champion of the Latin language, and has made no effort to hide that he loves to chant the Mass and occasionally to preach in Latin. Although still the official language of the Church and of Vatican City, Latin has largely fallen out of use both in the Mass and in ecclesiastical communications. Since 1978, Italian and Polish were more commonly used at the Vatican than Latin. Benedict has already indicated that he intends to return to the use of Latin in pontifical matters and in the celebration of the Mass. Unlike his three immediate predecessors, he gave his first blessing in Latin, read out his first homily to the cardinals in Latin, and celebrated the ordinary of the Mass in Latin. "There were tears in my eyes as I heard the Latin words absolving us of our venial sins and explicitly imploring for us the grace of final perseverance," wrote columnist Christopher Ferrara in the pages of *The Remnant*, a traditionalist Catholic newspaper that was very critical of the John Paul years. "What a joy it was to hear such words from the mouth of a Roman Pontiff again."[21]

In addition to the use of Latin, Pope Benedict seems to be consciously returning to many of the papal customs that had been lost since before Vatican II. In the days following the papal election, Roger McCaffery, founding editor of *Latin Mass* magazine predicted that with Pope Benedict "public

Masses with greetings of the flock in 21 languages may not be that common. Tight pronouncements in Latin (when speaking to churchmen) or just in Italian (when speaking to the faithful) will be the norm, or so it seems."[22]

—

Pope Benedict clearly favors the restoration of certain elements of the Mass that have been lost in the post-Vatican II scramble to reinvent Catholicism. Nevertheless, he is also sympathetic to those Catholics who prefer the traditional Latin rite of worship — the rite that was used in the Western Church for many centuries and codified in the years following the Council of Trent (and therefore often referred to as the "Tridentine Mass"). Indeed, he has endorsed the 1962 missal, the traditional Latin rite's last manifestation, as a legitimate and desirable option for the sacred liturgy. In October 1998, supporters of the traditional Latin Mass celebrated the tenth anniversary of Pope John Paul II's *Ecclesia Dei*, a pontifical exhortation that called on the world's Catholic bishops to make generous provision for those Catholics preferring celebrations of the old form of the Latin rite liturgy. One highlight of the tenth anniversary celebrations in Rome was an address by Cardinal Ratzinger to an audience of almost three thousand Catholics.

In his talk, he made clear that, although the Second Vatican Council ordered a reform of the liturgical rites, it did not prohibit the old rite. "The Church, throughout her history," he said, "has never forbidden or abolished orthodox liturgical forms."[23] In answer to objections that two different Latin rites are confusing and "disunifying," he explained that various Roman rites have always existed side by side, for example the Ambrosian, Mozarabic, Carthusian, Carmelite, and Dominican rites all coexisted in Europe in previous centuries.

Cardinal Ratzinger was also one of the very few cardinals who has celebrated the traditional Latin Mass in recent decades. On Easter Sunday in 1990, for example, he celebrated a pontifical High Mass at the International Seminary for the Fraternity of St. Peter, a religious society of priests devoted to the traditional Latin Mass. In 1999 he celebrated a pontifical High Mass in Weimer, Germany. The late Michael Davies, the Church's premiere defender of the Latin Mass in the decades following the Council, called Cardinal Ratzinger's Weimer Mass "a milestone in the campaign for the restoration of the Roman Missal of 1962 to the altars of the Church."[24]

The Society of St. Pius X, founded in 1969 in Switzerland by French-born Archbishop Marcel Lefebvre is the largest breakaway traditionalist group in the world, claiming some three million lay followers worldwide, thirty thousand of those in North America. Lefebvre publicly rejected the new Mass promulgated by Pope Paul VI in 1969. The traditionalist archbishop and his newly ordained priests were formally suspended seven years later and, in 1988, Lefebvre was excommunicated by Pope John Paul II for consecrating four bishops against the pope's orders. A few months later Archbishop Lefebvre and Cardinal Ratzinger appeared set to sign a protocol of reconciliation. The breakaway bishop, however, rejected the accord over a clause that gave the Vatican the last word on a commission designed to settle differences in the interpretation of the Council.

Since that time, the Vatican has considered the Society of St. Pius X in formal schism, though the group still professes to "maintain its loyalty to the papacy." Upon the election of Pope Benedict XVI, the society's Superior General, Bishop Bernard Fellay, welcomed the man who was Ratzinger in a statement issued on April 19, 2005, from its international headquarters in Menzinger, Switzerland, and professed "filial devotion" to the new pontiff. The bishop went on to say that, with the election of Joseph Ratzinger, he "sees a gleam of hope that we may find a way out of the profound crisis which is shaking the Catholic Church, of which some aspects have been spoken of by the former Head for the Congregation for the Doctrine of the Faith."[25]

In the final years of the John Paul pontificate many traditional Catholics increasingly voiced their desire for the Latin rite to be accorded its own "apostolic administration," that is, given its own hierarchy and made a distinct and separate rite of the Catholic Church, similar to that of the various Byzantine churches, each of which has its own bishops and priests who minister to the Church exclusively in their particular liturgical rite. A fruitful model for this has already been given in the provisions of reconciliation for the Society of St. Pius X in Campos, Brazil, under Bishop

Fernando Areas Rifan. The Apostolic Administration of Campos maintains its own churches and seminaries and ministers to thirty thousand Catholics.

—

In addition to restoring the liturgy, Pope Benedict XVI's "reform of the reform" also includes a veritable remodeling of the face of the Church through its sacred music, art, and architecture. His appreciation for sacred music is well known. A pianist himself, he once said that he is distrustful of theologians who "do not love art, poetry, music, nature: they can be dangerous."[26] Although the comment may come across as light and humorous, Cardinal Ratzinger was making a serious point: Those who cannot appreciate the artistic expression of the faith are often iconoclasts, who undermine Catholicism through their promotion of banality, reductionism, and fundamentalism. This strategy has produced a stripped down liturgy, barren church buildings, and a watering down of Catholic teaching in the decades following the Council. The result has been the secularization of the Church and obfuscation of Catholic identity.

— 9 —

Shedding the "Armor of Saul"

It is important that the nature and mission of the Church be taught in their entirety. The Church should be understood as more than a merely social entity, governed chiefly by psychological, sociological, and political processes. When it is viewed this way, its institutional or visible dimension is placed in opposition to its divine origin, mission and authority.

Joseph Cardinal Ratzinger, 1985[1]

As Cardinal Ratzinger, the future pope gave some indication that he is not only interested in remodeling the face of the Church, but the inner workings of its bureaucracy as well. Despite his reputation as an authoritarian, he is averse to the excessive bureaucracy that has characterized the Church in recent decades. While parishes and other Catholic institutions in many dioceses are closing or merging, the bureaucracies are growing as new committees and chancery offices are formed to address perceived challenges in the local or universal Church. "In the past two decades an excessive amount of institutionalization has come about in the Church, which is alarming," wrote the cardinal in his 1998 book *A New Song For the Lord*. "Future reforms should therefore aim not at the creation of yet more institutions, but at their reduction."[2] According to Sandro Magister, the religion editor for the Italian newspaper *L'Espresso*, Pope Benedict XVI would love to see a Church that is simpler in terms of bureaucracy: "He doesn't want its central and peripheral institutions—the Vatican curia, the diocesan chanceries, the episcopal conferences—to become 'like the armor of Saul, which prevented the young David from walking.'"[3]

Ratzinger believes that, like big government, these bureaucracies have become self-perpetuating and self-interested, incapable of serving the best interests of those to which they owe their responsibility and their existence. It would not be surprising then if the new pope initiates a reform of Church bureaucracies, including diocesan chanceries, national bishops conferences, and even the Roman Curia itself, all in the interest of shedding paperwork and returning to core pastoral concerns.

One important aspect of this "reform" is the relationship between the Vatican (and the authority of the papacy) and the national bishops conferences. For some time now, the

Church has been suffering under the weight of these ecclesiastical bodies. The United States Conference of Catholic Bishops (USCCB) provides a perfect example. In recent decades it has produced a mass of commissions, committees, and documents on every conceivable subject. Too often, however, the USCCB (formerly the NCCB) has served to undermine the Church's official positions as enunciated by the Vatican. It took the U.S. bishops committee on Catholic higher education a whole decade to study the implications of *Ex Corde Ecclessiae* before releasing its own guidelines for the document's implementation in the United States. These guidelines were criticized by the Vatican as inadequate.

Cardinal Ratzinger's 1986 document on "the pastoral care of homosexual persons," and his 1992 follow-up on "some considerations on legislation prohibiting discrimination against homosexual persons," was undermined by the USCCB when it released *Always Our Children*, another committee document that was found by the future pope to be deficient enough to require substantial revision before being reissued. The U.S. bishops did make the requested revisions and produced a new version of *Always Our Children*, but not before the initial version had already been distributed across the country and had become the primary text in homosexual discussion groups that were cropping up in dioceses across the country. Whereas the original version of *Always Our Children* was quoted with glee by "gay-lesbian activists," the same people denounced Cardinal Ratzinger as a "homophobe" for his reasoned disapproval of the original USCCB document on "ministry to lesbians and gays." Cardinal Ratzinger's 2004 letter to the U.S. bishops on withholding Communion from pro-abortion politicians suffered the same fate.

The bureaucratic process and the results it produces are a large part of the problem. The bishops conference receives the document from Rome, discusses it in an open forum at their semiannual meeting, forms a committee or group of committees to examine the topic in question, and only after considerable time passes, the committees draft their own interpretation of the Vatican document, making recommendations as to how it ought to be implemented in the United States given the country's "local circumstances." The committee recommendations are debated amongst the U.S. bishops before the committee or subcommittee releases its own document in final form. In some cases, such as that of the 1978 document "Environment and Art in Catholic Worship" (EACW), the documents are published by the subcommittee even without the approval of the full body of U.S. bishops. EACW recommended the iconoclastic renovation of Catholic churches—justifying the removal of pews, communion rails, statues, crucifixes, and other overt signs of Catholic devotion and expression. It was passed off as an authoritative presentation of Church teaching by the U.S. bishops, when it fact most of its directives contradicted the Second Vatican Council's Constitution on the Liturgy, which was supposed to be its inspiration.

Ratzinger recognized all these problems only too well and sought to reign in some of the abuses by bishops conferences with the release of his 1998 document *Apostolos Suos*. He sought not only to redefine the nature and understanding of bishops conferences, he also argued they had no teaching authority of their own. Signed by Pope John Paul II, *Apostolos Suos* declared that national episcopal conferences were not an expression of collegiality, but derived their authority solely from their unity with the pope. Therefore, these national conferences could not issue statements on moral or doctrinal matters unless they were approved unanimously or had prior approval from the Vatican. Many regarded this as a classic exercise of raw political power. In fact it was a reasonable clarification of a confusing matter in the Church, one that Cardinal Ratzinger and Pope John Paul thought could threaten to reduce the Catholic Church to a loose federation of local or national churches, similar to the Anglican communion.

—

Although Ratzinger believes in shedding the layers of bureaucracy, he is keenly aware that the Supreme Pontiff has the trifold mandate to teach, to sanctify, and to rule in the name of Christ. His predecessor took the first two mandates to heart: he taught and he sanctified. But by his own admission he failed, at least in some respects, in his obligation to rule. Pope John Paul's passion for travel and dialogue sometimes meant a certain neglect of internal administration of the Church. According to George Weigel's authorized biography of the late pope, Cardinal Wojtyla had much the same problem as archbishop of Krakow. Administration—ruling—was not his strong point.[4]

Pope Benedict has different ideas and different strengths. He is much less likely to be away from the Vatican and the central affairs of the Church than his predecessor, not only because of his age, but because of his style. He will undoubtedly take closer control of the internal workings of the Vatican.

Perhaps the most important aspect of this papal obligation is the nomination of bishops and the appointment of cardinals who function as the pope's closest advisors. Few would argue that John Paul's appointments were not nearly as bad as those of Pope Paul VI. The Montini papacy revolutionized the hierarchy through the elevation of out-and-out renegades to the episcopacy. In the United States, on the recommendation of the extreme liberal papal delegate Archbishop Jean Jadot[5] of Belgium, a number of stridently anti-Roman clerics were advanced into positions of great authority. For example, during Jadot's time in Washington, 1973 to 1980, Raymond Hunthausen was promoted to archbishop of Seattle, Rembert Weakland to archbishop of Milwaukee, Raymond Lucker to bishop of New Ulm, and Howard Hubbard to bishop of Albany, even though Hubbard was just thirty-nine years old at the time.

Nevertheless, many appointments were remarkably bad from 1978 to 2004, especially considering John Paul's reputation for orthodoxy and his concern for episcopal fortitude. Contrary to the oft-repeated belief that Karol Wojtyla appointed men who were near-facsimiles of himself, Benedict's predecessor gave the world Cardinals Roger Mahony of Los Angeles, Joseph Bernardin of Chicago, Keith O'Brien of Scotland, Godfried Daneels of Belgium, and Karl Lehmann of Mainz—all of whom have (or had) reputations as extremely liberal archbishops and have had significant influence over the choice of other bishops in their respective countries.

Another notable problem is the large number of troublesome homosexual bishops appointed on John Paul's watch. In the U.S., for example, he appointed Patrick Zeiman, Daniel Ryan, Kendrick Williams, Keith Symons, and Anthony O'Connell, all of whom were disgraced by homosexual scandals. According to an unnamed Vatican source and reported by columnist Jack Wheeler, "whenever Vatican investigators brought the results of their vetting process regarding an individual's candidacy for bishop . . . and they revealed he was a homosexual, John Paul II would refuse to believe it." Accusing a man of homosexuality was a standard tactic used by the former Communist government of his native Poland in order to discredit their "enemies of the state." From his ordination to the priesthood following the Second World War until 1963 when he was consecrated archbishop of Krakow, he witnessed this personal destruction repeatedly. "So traumatized," explained Wheeler, "he summarily dismissed such accusations as Pope, and would approve the elevation of anyone so accused."[6]

John Paul, of course, did not and could not personally know every one of the bishops he appointed during his twenty-six year pontificate. He relied heavily on his cardinals and their national bishops' conferences to recommend the best men for each position. The process leading up to the appointment of bishops includes a secretive vetting process that Cardinal Ratzinger was all too familiar with, being a prominent member of the Vatican's Congregation for Bishops.

Bishops put forward names of priests who they believe would make good episcopal leaders. According to Vatican norms, bishops must enjoy a good reputation; be of irreproachable morality; be endowed with right judgment and prudence; have an even temper and be of stable character. They are expected to exercise their pastoral ministry with zeal, piety, and in a spirit of sacrifice. Above all, they must hold firmly to the orthodox faith and be devoted to the Holy See. These, however, are not common traits of the typical bishop, at least not in the U.S. In recent times, we have seen that all too many bishops are incompetent, ill-mannered, and gravely immoral.

This is the situation that Pope Benedict XVI has inherited. As Cardinal Ratzinger he was generally regarded as a good judge of character and has already become familiar with many of the potential candidates for the episcopacy through his work at the Congregation for Bishops. Furthermore, given his suspicion of the national bishops' conferences and his previous experiences with the United States bishops conference, some hope that the new pope may even reform the selection process of bishops. The current process has proved a failure. It is an especially difficult situation since, once a bishop is appointed it is very difficult to remove him from office.

—

The case of Raymond "Dutch" Hunthausen provides an illustrative example. Archbishop Hunthausen, the youngest American bishop to attend the Second Vatican Council, was named archbishop of Seattle in 1975. Even before he arrived in Washington state, he had earned a reputation as a political activist and episcopal rebel. As bishop of Helena in his home state of Montana, he was an inveterate pacifist and anti-nuclear protestor. He made news for, among other tactics, lying across the railroad tracks in order to block a train carrying arms parts for the manufacture of a nuclear reactor. He refused to pay his taxes, in protest against the U.S. military's stance in Vietnam. He was truly a "polarizing" figure. Many loved him; many hated him.

But as extreme as his political positions and protests were, his approach to shepherding the Catholic Church in the American northwest was even more extreme. Under his tutelage, the archdiocese of Seattle turned into a "liberal playground in matters of Catholic discipline."[7] His critics say he was out to remake the Catholic Church in his own image—and few would argue he did not succeed.

After receiving years of complaints about the Archdiocese of Seattle at the Vatican, Cardinal Ratzinger initiated an investigation to evaluate criticisms about Hunthausen's ministry as archbishop. In 1983 he appointed Cardinal James Hickey of Washington, D.C., as an "apostolic visitor." Two years later, in 1985, Ratzinger released the findings of the investigation. He wrote that "there has been a rather widespread practice of admitting divorced persons to a subsequent Church marriage without prior review by your Tribunal, or even after they have received a negative sentence."[8] Other problems were doctrinal: incorrect notions of the Church's mission, flawed understandings of the dignity of the human person, and even problems with the teaching on Christ's divinity, humanity, and His salvific mission. Archbishop Hunthausen was also criticized for failing to impart "a correct appreciation of the sacramental nature of the Church, especially as it provides for sacred ministry in the Sacrament of Holy Orders," and instructed that he needed to establish a seminary program which would "inculcate the candidates for the priesthood an understanding of the sacraments as the Lord's gifts to His Church."[9]

The list of criticisms went on and on, a veritable syllabus of errors that might have been uncovered to some degree in many U.S. dioceses, especially at that time: contraceptive sterilization was routinely taking place in local Catholic hospitals; first Communion was offered before first Confession; the practice of general absolution was abused; intercommunion was common practice at Seattle parishes; laicized priests were serving in unauthorized priestly roles; priests who had unlawfully left the priesthood (and their civilly married wives) were employed by the Archdiocese; the possibility of women's ordination was being promoted; and homosexual activist groups received diocesan support.[10]

One of the most controversial aspects of Hunthausen's ministry was his zealous support of "homosexual rights." In 1977, the Seattle archbishop gave his imprimatur to Jesuit Fr. Philip S. Keane's book *Sexual Morality: A Catholic Perspective*. Despite the fact that an imprimatur is a bishop's guarantee that a text is free from doctrinal and moral error, Keane's book openly transgressed Catholic teaching by endorsing homosexual unions even to the point of justifying homosexual intercourse and "heavy petting" for Catholic priests, despite their promise of celibacy. It is instructive to note that Fr. Keane was rector of Seattle's St. Thomas Seminary at the time (and later went on to serve as vice-rector of St. Mary's Seminary in Baltimore).[11]

In 1983, Hunthausen invited the militant homosexual group Dignity to meet at Seattle's St. James Cathedral. Dignity, a nationwide group of Catholics who openly protest and dissent from the Church's teachings on homosexuality held "gay-lesbian" Masses there that have been described as "sacrilegious."[12] Hunthausen defended the Dignity meeting by saying that "they're Catholics, too. They need a place to pray."[13] A weekly Dignity Mass, advertised in the Seattle Gay News, also took place at St. Joseph's Church until 1988. For years the parish served as the epicenter for the homosexual rights movement in Seattle. In 1987, for example, it was the site of the "Gay Pride Kick-Off Dance" that opened Gay Pride Week in the city that year.

After Hunthausen came under fire by the Vatican, Fr. James Jorgenson, the chaplain for Seattle's Dignity chapter (who later left the priesthood), wrote a letter to the editor of the *National Catholic Reporter* defending his archbishop: "Raymond Hunthausen has clearly given voice to the Gospel's invitation that all people love themselves as their neighbors. With his faithful assistance, the Spirit of God herself has convinced my friends at Dignity of their goodness. No magisterial pronouncement will ever undercut the Good News."[14]

In short, the archbishop's "ministry to homosexuals" consisted of affirming their homosexual inclinations and activities, providing the "gay community" a place to meet regularly—in the name of the Catholic Church. Despite evidence to contrary as well as Dignity's consistent and loud denunciation of the Church's official teaching on homosexuality, Hunthausen maintained all along that he was being faithful to the teachings of the Church.

In January of 1986, Cardinal Ratzinger directed that Hunthausen delegate all his final decision-making authority over five areas of church life—annulments, clergy formation, resigned priests, liturgy and moral issues dealing with homosexuals and hospitals—to a Vatican-appointed auxiliary bishop. Bishop Donald Wuerl (later Bishop of Pittsburgh) was a catechetical specialist sent to Seattle because Cardinal Ratzinger did not have confidence that Archbishop Hunthausen could—or would—implement the necessary reforms. The appointment was not announced publicly, and

Archbishop Hunthausen was not otherwise disciplined or censured. Cardinal Ratzinger had deliberately acted slowly and discreetly, not wishing to humiliate the American rebel. Archbishop Hunthausen wasn't removed from office, nor was he reprimanded publicly or privately. He was merely given an auxiliary bishop, whose duty would be to see to it that the archdiocese would receive proper pastoral guidance and proper administration.

It was the archbishop himself who created the very public "Hunthausen Affair," as it was called. Two months before a meeting of the NCCB, Hunthausen complained openly and bitterly, appealing to his liberal supporters in Seattle, his fellow U.S. bishops, and above all to the media, who proved to be a very supportive voice, even calling Wuerl's appointment "vindictive." The *Seattle Post-Intelligencer* portrayed the Vatican investigation as "secretive" and "unjust." After all, Hunthausen had been championing their favorite causes—feminism, homosexuality, moral and religious liberalism and so forth—for nearly a decade at the time.

In Archbishop Hunthausen's self-absorbed view, he regarded himself as nothing short of a martyr. Cardinal Ratzinger's investigation was unfair, he contended. Rome had no right to "butt in" on the affairs of his diocese, he chimed over and over in media interviews, despite the fact that his authority as archbishop of Seattle came solely from Rome.

In the hierarchy, Hunthausen's most vocal supporter was Milwaukee's Archbishop Rembert Weakland, who was later disgraced for a sordid homosexual relationship he had with a theology student. Archbishop Weakland ran his archdiocese in very much the same way as Archbishop Hunthausen ran Seattle, even down to the specifics of allowing militant homosexual groups to meet at his cathedral, which became a "cruising center" in downtown Milwaukee. At the national bishops' meeting in Washington in November 1986, Weakland likened Cardinal Ratzinger's investigation to "the Inquisition and the periodic witch hunts for heretics."[15] Accordingly, press reports bristled with references to the Inquisition, confusing the Holy Office of the Inquisition (the former name for Cardinal Ratzinger's Congregation for the Doctrine of the Faith) with the Spanish Inquisition.

In a statement released to media at the end of the bishops' conference, Hunthausen complained he had never been able to confront his "accusers" or to see the "allegations" against him. He admitted that he may have made some errors in "pastoral judgment" and, here and there, made an "oversight." But contrary to all the evidence examined by Cardinal Ratzinger's office, he denied that he had ever rejected Catholic teaching or intended to defy the Vatican. Just as theologians who deny the divinity of Christ insist that they are Catholic theologians in good standing, Archbishop Hunthausen was insisting that he had, all along, been acting responsibly in his duty as shepherd of the Seattle archdiocese. Although Cardinal Ratzinger had investigated whether the Catholics of northwest Washington were getting proper pastoral guidance and the sound teaching they were entitled to, the archbishop tuned the affair into an "unfair trial" that violated his personal rights.

The press took their cues from Hunthausen and cast Cardinal Ratzinger in the role of Torquemada in the affair. In a front page story, The *Washington Post* called the future Pope Benedict the inheritor of "the mantle of the grand inquisitor of the Middle Ages," suggesting that Hunthausen was going to be burnt at the stake.[16]

The Hunthausen Affair forced the U.S. bishops to release a statement affirming their "unreserved loyalty to and unity with the Holy Father." Although Archbishop Hunthausen received many expressions of sympathy from his fellow bishops, the statement from the conference president Bishop James Malone admitted that "the conference of bishops has no authority to intervene in the internal affairs of a diocese or in the unique relationship between the Pope and individual bishops."[17]

Archbishop Hunthausen, however, was not content to let matters rest. He continued in his campaign to advance himself as the Martyr of Seattle, a campaign that caused no little problem for newly consecrated Auxiliary Bishop Donald Wuerl. The archbishop was particularly upset that Bishop Wuerl would have final authority over important areas of diocesan life including the marriage tribunal, liturgy, priestly formation, and ministry to homosexuals. In a move meant to show support for the beleaguered Hunthausen, personnel at the Archdiocese of Seattle would not allow Bishop Wuerl into his office at the chancery or provide him with a place to stay.

The archbishop created an uproar and convinced his priests and laity that he was the victim of "right wing groups" [sic] like Catholics United for the Faith and the *Wanderer*, a lay-run Catholic news weekly that had published a series of articles detailing Hunthausen's abuses. The articles culminated in the 1992 book *The Hunthausen File* by Wanderer contributor Gary Bullert.

A well-organized campaign by Hunthausen supporters—bishops, priests, nuns and some lay Catholics—created a whirlwind of media exposure that served to demonize Cardinal Ratzinger (the "villain") and beatify Hunthausen (the "hero"). The archbishop found the press to be an effective public relations tool for himself, judging from erroneous reports that regularly issued forth from mainstream media organs like the *Seattle Times*, which consistently reported that the Vatican had publicized the affair in order to humiliate Hunthausen, when it was the archbishop himself who had initiated the publicity. "Cardinal Ratzinger seems determined to push the church backward to dinosaurlike extinction," a *Seattle Times* letter writer opined in 1986.

Therefore, the Hunthausen Affair had an unexpected twist of an ending: the Vatican removed Bishop Wuerl from Seattle and restored Hunthausen's full authority over the archdiocese, where he remained, continuing on with the same abuses of doctrine and discipline, until he retired in 1991 at the age of seventy, five years before the mandatory retirement age for bishops.

Judging from the reaction to the election of Benedict XVI to the papacy, some clerics in Seattle are still enraged by the man who was Ratzinger. Fr. Michael G. Ryan was Hunthausen's vicar general and referred to the archbishop's tenure in Seattle as "a Camelot moment." At the time of the April 2005 conclave, Fr. Ryan was pastor of Seattle's St. James Cathedral. He made no attempt to hide his disappointment. Although two decades had passed since Cardinal Ratzinger issued his report to Archbishop Hunthausen, Fr. Ryan said in a homily the day after the election that Cardinal Ratzinger was not what he "expected or even wanted."[18]

Truly, for many Catholic reformers, Pope Benedict XVI was not what they "expected or even wanted." Many "progressive" Catholics are already longing for the days of John Paul II, a pontiff they once took every opportunity to skewer when he upheld the faith of the Church. To be sure, few popes have begun their papacy with so many enemies lying in wait as Benedict XVI has.

No doubt the international secular press will remain hostile to the Ratzinger papacy. After all, Pope Benedict is a man with fixed beliefs that stand in stark opposition to their typically relativist worldview. The pope is their direct critic, and many in the secular press have marked Benedict as their enemy, a point that comes as little surprise. The same, however, can be said about the Catholic Left, the arm of the Church that wants to adapt the teachings and practices of Catholicism to the ways of the world.

The high profile dismissal of Fr. Thomas Reese, SJ, as editor of the Jesuit-run *America* magazine in the earliest days of the Benedict pontificate illustrates this conflict. Technically, the priest resigned from his position as editor at the request of his religious superiors. As reported in the *New York Times* and other venues, however, the Jesuits presented Fr. Reese's departure as a "forced ouster" effected by the Congregation for the Doctrine of the Faith shortly before Cardinal Ratzinger was elected to the papacy. The *National Catholic Reporter* characterized the personnel change at *America* as the result of a five-year exchange between Ratzinger's CDF and the Jesuits and Fr. Reese. [19] During that time, the Vatican reportedly received complaints about Reese's editorial policies from certain unnamed bishops in the United States. They raised objections to Reese's choice of material including articles that called into question the Church's teachings on issues such as contraception, religious pluralism, homosexual unions, and stem cell research. Fr. Reese's *America* was also notably a vocal critic of Ratzinger's CDF, especially in regard to the Vatican's investigation of Catholic theologians.

Though it is not known to what degree Ratzinger was personally involved with the Reese case, the media generally presented the "forced ouster" as the final act of the man who was Ratzinger as well as the first significant act of

Pope Benedict XVI. Not a few media outlets, both Catholic and mainstream, characterized the personnel change at *America* as the result of a cruel inquisition and an augury of an intolerably dictatorial papacy. The lay-run American Catholic weekly *Commonweal*, for example, editorialized that Fr. Reese's removal leaves the impression that the Catholic Church is "a backward-looking, essentially authoritarian, institution run by men who are afraid of open debate and intellectual inquiry."[20]

Obviously this type of hyperbole and suspicion about Pope Benedict XVI is not going to go away. It is merely another indicator of the culture wars that are taking place both within the Church and without. If, however, Fr. Reese's dismissal was indeed the first act of a new Vatican policy, it is imperative that the bishops and the Catholic media be able to explain to the general public just how reasonable such actions are. To be sure, the departure of Fr. Reese from *America* is significant and important. He was not only the editor of an influential Jesuit-run and Church-sanctioned periodical, he was also a primary source of background information for secular reporters writing on issues involving the Catholic Church. Having authored several books about the Church hierarchy, he has long been regarded as one of America's most knowledgeable Church insiders.

The former editor is the classic accommodationist of the Catholic Left. While never formally dissenting from Church teaching, through his editorial policies he has consistently called the Church's teachings into question under the guise of "intellectual inquiry"—a disingenuous modus operandi at best, especially for someone who describes himself as an intellectual. For example, in an April 25, 2005 editorial in *America* entitled "Challenges for the New Pope," Fr. Reese called for an "open discussion" of "birth control, divorce, women priests.... homosexuality," and so forth, in an obvious attempt to lobby for a change in the Catholic understanding of those issues—issues that are, significantly, the politically fashionable topics of the day. He wrote: "The pope will ... face a growing population of educated Catholic women who feel alienated from the church.... Losing educated women in the 21st century will be ... problematic, since it is most often women who pass on the faith to the next generation as educators and mothers.... Women's ordination must be open for discussion." In calling for this "open discussion," Fr. Reese suggested that by not putting these hot-button issues of the Catholic Left on the table for discussion, the Catholic Church is "on the wrong side of history."

Commenting in the *Boston Globe*, Fr. Richard John Neuhaus, editor of *First Things*, explained the problem with Reese's editorial policy, given that *America* is a Church-sanctioned media outlet: "It was thought that being 'fair and balanced' required publishing on an equal footing articles that opposed the church's teaching, as though the church's teaching was but one opinion among others. The problem was compounded by the fact that such articles dealt with publicly controversial questions such as the moral understanding of homosexuality, same-sex marriage, and the exploitation of embryonic stem cells."[21] Fr. Reese's departure is just as reasonable as the sacking of an editor working for Planned Parenthood who consistently published articles that opposed or undermined the mission of the organization. As Fr. Neuhaus pointed out, "there is a problem if an editor is in fundamental disagreement with the institution for which he works."[22]

If the Reese case, overblown as it was, is truly an indication of how the man who was Ratzinger will steer the Catholic Church during his pontificate, many rank and file practicing Catholics will no doubt rejoice in the strong papacy, a point that continues to go unreported. Pope Benedict XVI is a man who is respected as an eminent theologian, a brilliant intellect, and a perceptive person. He has set an agenda for himself that is ambitious, but attainable. As with the agenda of any pope, it will naturally have its opponents both within the Church and without. Without a doubt, the papacy of Pope Benedict XVI will go down in history as one of tremendous significance. Whatever the Holy Father does it is likely to carry weight for many decades to come.

A Brief Chronology of Joseph Ratzinger, Pope Benedict XVI

1927: Born on April 16, Holy Saturday, in Marktrl-am-Inn, Bavaria.

1951: Ordained to the priesthood on June 29 by Cardinal Faulhaber.

1953: Receives doctorate in theology from the University of Munich.

1962-1965: Advisor to Cardinal Frings, Archbishop of Cologne, at the Second Vatican Council.

1968: Publishes *Introduction to Christianity*, his first major work.

1972: Co-founds the theological journal *Communio*.

1977: Episcopal ordination on May 28, archbishop of Munich and Freising. Nominated cardinal by Pope Paul VI on June 27.

1981: Named prefect of the Congregation for the Doctrine of the Faith by Pope John Paul II.

1985: Publishes *The Ratzinger Report*, a book length interview with Italian journalist Vittorio Messori.

2005: Elected Pope Benedict XVI on April 19 by the Sacred College of Cardinals.

Works by Joseph Ratzinger
(available in English)

BOOKS

1968: *Introduction to Christianity*
Ratzinger's first major work demonstrates that the place for the Christian faith is in the Catholic Church. His elucidation of the Apostle's Creed gives an thorough interpretation of the foundations of Christianity.

1985: *The Ratzinger Report*
Ratzinger speaks candidly and forcefully about the state of the Church in the post-Vatican II era. He provides a clear and uncompromising report on the dangers that threaten the faith.

1986: *The Feast of Faith*
A collection of essays in which Ratzinger presents "approaches to the theology of the liturgy."

1986: *Principles of Christian Morality*
A compendium of the fundamental principles of Christian life, co-written with Hans Urs Von Balthasar.

1987: *Behold the Pierced One*
Proceeding from the prayerful dialogue between Jesus and His Eternal Father, Ratzinger shows how one can only approach the mystery of the Heart of Christ through the imitation of His prayer.

1987: *Principles of Catholic Theology*
A collection of articles in which Ratzinger outlines the fundamental principles of theology and the proper relationship of theology to Church teaching and authority.

1989: *Eschatology: Death and Eternal Life*
Ratzinger unites recent emphasis on the theology of hope for a future with traditional elements of the doctrine—heaven and hell, purgatory, death, and the immortality of the soul.

1990: *In the Beginning . . . : A Catholic Understanding of the Story of Creation and the Fall*
Ratzinger discusses God as creator, the meaning of the biblical creation accounts, the creation of human beings, sin and salvation, and the consequences of faith in creation.

1992: *Co-Workers of the Truth*
Ratzinger offers selected passages from his profound spiritual and theological writings as meditations for each day of the year.

1993: *Meaning of Christian Brotherhood*
Written over three decades ago, Ratzinger's profound treatise on the true meaning of Christian brotherhood is a clear statement on the biblical grounds for cooperation among believing Christians.

1994: *Turning Point for Europe*
Ratzinger addresses the challenges and responsibilities that

both the Church and society in Europe face after the collapse of Marxism.

1994: *Introduction to the Catechism of the Catholic Church*
As head of the Bishops Commission for the Implementation of the Catechism, Ratzinger provides helpful insights on how to read and study the *Catechism*. Co-written with Cardinal Christoph Schoenborn.

1995: *Nature and Mission of Theology*
Written in response to the "dialogue" going on today concerning theology and the clarification of its methods, its mission and its limits.

1996: *Called to Communion: Understanding the Church Today*
Ratzinger examines a number of important issues such as the need of papal primacy to ensure Christian unity; the true meaning of the priesthood as a sacrament and not a mere ministry; and the role of the bishops as successors of the Apostles.

1996: *A New Song for the Lord*
Ratzinger addresses the critical issues of the correct form of worship, sacred music, and the important relationship of Christology and liturgy.

1997: *Gospel, Catechesis, Catechism: Sidelights on the Catechism of the Catholic Church*
Ratzinger offers insights on the catechetical character and biblical foundation of the *Catechism of the Catholic Church*.

1997: *Salt of the Earth*
A book-length interview with a journalist Peter Seewald on a host of controversial and difficult issues facing Catholicism and Christianity at the end of the millennium.

1998: *Milestones: Memoirs 1927–1977*
Ratzinger's autobiography, peppered with theological insights.

1999: *Many Religions, One Covenant*
Ratzinger presents a biblical theology to deepen our understanding of the Bible's most fundamental principle—the covenant.

2000: *The Spirit of the Liturgy*
Ratzinger's book-length examination of contemporary problems surrounding the celebration of the liturgy and outlines his proposed "reform of the reform."

2002: *God and the World: Believing and Living in Our Time*
Ratzinger's second book-length interview with journalist Peter Seewald in which he addresses deep questions of faith and the living of that faith in the modern world.

2003: *God Is Near Us: The Eucharist, the Heart of Life*
Ratzinger demonstrates the biblical, historical, and theological dimensions of the Eucharist.

2004: *Truth and Tolerance: Christian Belief and World Religions*
Describing the vast array of world religions, Ratzinger embraces the difficult challenge of meeting diverse understandings of spiritual truth while defending the Catholic teaching of salvation through Jesus Christ.

2005: *Pilgrim Fellowship of Faith: The Church as Communion*
A collection of essays, lectures, letters, and conferences that Ratzinger has written in recent years on issues of theology, the modern world, secularism, non-Christian religions, and other key topics of the Catholic Church.

2005: *Values in a Time of Upheaval*
Ratzinger's critique of relativism presented with chapters on the history and destiny of human life, the dangers of secularism, the meaning of truth in a pluralistic world, morality, and the Christian basis for hope.

DOCTRINAL DOCUMENTS AUTHORIZED BY JOSEPH RATZINGER AT THE CONGREGATION AT THE DOCTRINE OF THE FAITH

December 2004: Notification regarding the book *Jesus Symbol of God* of Fr Roger Haight, SJ.

July 2004: Letter to the bishops of the Catholic Church on the collaboration of men and women in the Church and in the world.

July 2003: Considerations regarding proposals to give legal recognition to unions between homosexual persons.

January 2003: Doctrinal note on some questions regarding the participation of Catholics in political life.

July 2001: Note on the force of the doctrinal decrees concerning the thought and work of Fr Antonio Rosmini Serbati.

February and May 2001: Notification regarding certain writings of Fr. Marciano Vidal, CSSR.

January 2001: Notification on the book *Toward a Christian Theology of Religious Pluralism* by Fr. Jacques Dupuis, SJ.

November 2000: Notification concerning some writings of Professor Dr. Reinhard Messner.

September 2000: Instruction on prayers for healing.

August 2000: *Dominus Iesus*—Declaration on the unicity and salvific universality of Jesus Christ and the Church.

June 2000: Note on the expression "Sister Churches."

June 2000: Documents regarding "The Message of Fatima."

May 1999: Notification regarding Sister Jeannine Gramick, SSND, and Father Robert Nugent, SDS.

October 1998: Considerations on "The Primacy of the successor of Peter in the ministry of the Church."

June 1998: Formula to be used for the profession of faith and for the oath of fidelity to assume an office to be exercised in the name of the Church.

June 1998: Notification concerning the writings of Fr. Anthony De Mello, SJ.

January 1997: Notification on the book *Mary and Human Liberation* by Fr. Tissa Balasuriya, OMI.

October 1995: Notification on the writings and activities of Mrs. Vassula Ryden.

July 1993: Responses to questions proposed concerning uterine isolation and related matters .

July 1992: "Some Considerations Concerning the Response to Legislative Proposals on Non-discrimination of Homosexual Persons."

June 1992: Decree on the doctrine and customs of the Association "Opus Angelorum."

May 1992: *Communionis notio*—Letter to the bishops of the Catholic Church on some aspects of the Church understood as Communion.

March 1992: Instruction on some aspects of the use of the instruments of social communication in promoting the doctrine of the faith.

January 1992: Note on the book *The Sexual Creators, An Ethical Proposal for Concerned Christians* by Fr. André Guindon, OMI.

May 1990: *Donum veritatis*—Instruction on the ecclesial vocation of the theologian.

October 1989: *Orationis formas*—Letter on certain aspects of the Christian meditation

February 1989: Note regarding "The moral rule of *Humanae vitae* and the pastoral duty."

November 1988: Observations on ARCIC II's "Salvation and the Church."

July 1988: Formula to be used for the profession of faith and for the oath of fidelity to assume an office to be exercised in the name of the Church.

February 1987: *Donum vitae*—Instruction on respect for human life in its origin and on the dignity of procreation.

October 1986: *Homosexualitatis problema*—Letter to the bishops of the Catholic Church on the pastoral care of homosexual persons.

September 1986: Notification on the book *Pleidooi voor mensen in de Kerk* by Edward Schillebeeckx, OP.

September 1986: Letter to György Bulányi on certain writings attributed to him.

July 1986: Letter regarding the suspension of Charles Curran from the teaching of theology.

March 1986: *Libertatis conscientia*—Instruction on Christian freedom and liberation.

March 1985: Notification on the book *Church: Charism and Power. Essay on Militant Ecclesiology* by Father Leonardo Boff, OFM.

August 1984: *Libertatis nuntius*—Instruction on certain aspects of the "theology of liberation."

June 1984: Letter to Father Edward Schillebeeckx regarding his book *Ministry in the Church*.

December 1983: Decisions on the translation of the article "Carnis resurrectionem" of the Apostolic Symbol.

September 1983: Letter to Cardinal Joseph Höffner, archbishop of Cologne, regarding Opus Angelorum.

May 1983: Notification regarding Rev. Georges de Nantes.

March 1982: Letter to H.E. Msgr. Alan C. Clark regarding the final report of the Anglican Roman Catholic International Commission.

Notes

Introduction: A Different Kind of Pendulum Papacy

1 "Concerns New Pope Is Hardliner," CBS News, April 19, 2005.
2 Dooley, Tara. "World reacts to new pope, Benedict XVI," *Houston Chronicle*, April 19, 2005.
3 "German Reception of New Pope Mixed," *Deutsche Welle*, April 19, 2005.
4 Chittister, Joan. "And he shall be called . . ." *National Catholic Reporter*, April 20, 2005.

1 *The Beseiged Soul of Christian Europe*

1 Ratzinger, Joseph (Benedict XVI). *Values in a Time of Upheaval*, New York: Crossroad Publishing Company, 2005.
2 Ratzinger, Joseph Cardinal. "Relativism: The Central Problem for Faith Today," address to the presidents of the Doctrinal Commissions of the Bishops' Conferences of Latin America, Guadalajara, Mexico, May, 1996.
3 Ratzinger, Joseph Cardinal. Homily at the Mass opening the April 2005, conclave.
4 Ibid.
5 Ibid.

6 Ratzinger, Joseph Cardinal. Address at Subiaco (hometown of St. Benedict, patron of Europe), April 1, 2005.

7 Ibid.

8 Ratzinger, Joseph Cardinal. "Europe: Its Spiritual Foundations of Yesterday, Today, and Tomorrow," address at the library of the Italian Senate, Sala Capitolare del Chiostro della Minerva, May 13, 2004.

9 Pope John Paul II. Angelus homily, Castel Gandolfo, July 20, 2003.

10 Comment by Jacques Chirac to *Le Figaro*. English translation provided by John L. Allen, "Word From Rome," *National Catholic Reporter*, January 31, 2003.

11 Cross, Simon. "Chirac says 'No' to God in constitution," Institute on Religion and Public Policy, February 3, 2003.

12 Ratzinger Joseph Cardinal. Address to the Center for Political Orientation, Rome, October 25, 2004.

13 Ratzinger, Joseph Cardinal. Address at Subiaco (hometown of St. Benedict, patron of Europe), April 1, 2005.

14 Ibid.

15 This was Buttiglione's answer to a question from a Polish delegate. The question was "In your opinion, is marriage a relationship between a man and a woman, or perhaps something different?"

16 "Buttiglione regrets slur on gays," BBC News, October 21, 2004. Apropos the title of the BBC headline, Buttiglione did not regret what he had said. In a letter to Commission President Jose Manuel Barroso, Buttiglione wrote: "I deeply regret the difficulties and problems that have arisen."

17 As reported by *Deutsche Welle*, "Fate of Incoming EU Commission Still Uncertain," October 22, 2004.

18 Ambrosio, Gianni. "On the future of Catholicism in France," *L'Espresso*, May 9, 2005.

19 Ratzinger, Joseph Cardinal. Address at Subiaco (hometown of St. Benedict, patron of Europe), April 1, 2005.

20 The original German-language edition was published as *Salz der Erde*.

2 *The "Ideology of Dialogue"*

1 Ratzinger, Joseph Cardinal. Press conference address introducing *Dominus Iesus*, September 5, 2000.

2 "Confessions of a Cardinal," Interview of Cardinal Silvio Oddi by Tommasco Ricci, *30 Days*, November, 1990, p. 64.

3 Magister, Sandro. "Disputed Questions—Like Salvation Outside of the Church," July 16, 2003.

4 In a September 21, 1986 Angelus Address, John Paul thanked "all those of the Christian Churches and of the other great religions of the world, who have accepted the invitation to go to Assisi on 27 October, for a special meeting of prayer for peace, today so fragile and threatened."

5 *Redemptor Hominis*, March 4, 1979, John Paul II.

6 Ibid., no. 36.

7 *Dominus Iesus*, Congregation for the Doctrine of the Faith, August 2000.

8 Allen, John L. "Exclusive claim," *National Catholic Reporter*, Sept. 15, 2000.

9 "Vatican impedes interfaith dialogue," Spirituality Justice, Call to Action USA, October, 2000.

10 Allen, John L. "Exclusive claim," *National Catholic Reporter*, Sept. 15, 2000.

11 "Martini voices some reservations on Vatican text," *Tablet*, Sept. 16, 2000.

12 "Dismay, Disdain Over Vatican Document," *New York Times*, Sept. 6, 2000.

13 *Dominus Iesus*, no. 6.

14 "Latest bump in contradictory papacy," *National Catholic Reporter*, Sept. 15, 2000.

15 "Cardinal Mahony pledges 'unyielding support' to dialogue partners," Catholic News Service, Sept. 12, 2000.

16 Chirico, Peter. "Dominus Iesus as an event," America, March 26, 2001.

17 Contreras, Rodrigo. "A reflection on the dialogue between the Roman Catholic and Anglican Churches," Anglicans Online, October 2000.

18 Statement by the Archbishop of Canterbury concerning the Roman Catholic document *Dominus Iesus*," Lambeth Palace, Sept. 5, 2000.

19 Allen, John L. "Ratzinger speaks out in new book, debate," *National Catholic Reporter*, Oct. 6, 2000.

20 Magister, Sandro. "At the Right Hand of the Father: Ratzinger Promotes His Star Pupil," *L'Espresso*, Jan. 2, 2003.

21 Norton, John. "Missionary official says Vatican document recalls core teachings," Catholic News Service, Sept. 6, 2000.

22 "World Methodist Council leaders respond to Vatican document," United Methodist News Service, Sept., 2000.

23 "In Assisi, Religions Will Resolve Not to Use God to Justify Violence," Zenit News Agency, Jan. 18, 2002.

24 Ratzinger, Joseph Cardinal. *Truth and Tolerance: Christian Belief and World Religions*, (translated into English by Henry Taylor), San Francisco: Ignatius Press, 2003.

25 "A distinction must be made between multireligious and interreligious prayer," Zenit News Agency, Oct. 2, 2003.

26 *Redemptoris Missio*, no. 6.

3 *Islam and the Crisis of Christian Identity*

1 de Ravinel, Sophie. Interview with Joseph Cardinal Ratzinger, *Le Figaro*, Aug. 13, 2004.

2 Taheri, Amir. "Vatican's Ties With Islam," *Arab News*, April 16, 2005.

3 Guolo, Renzo. "John Paul II's Vision of the Church and Islam," *L'Espresso*, Sept. 8, 2003.

4 Ibid.

5 Ibid.

6 William, Daniel and Cooperman, Alan. "Vatican rethinking relations with Islam," *Washington Post*, Apr. 16, 2005.

7 From a speech delivered at Velletri, Italy as reported by *Il Giornale del Popolo*, Sept. 20, 2004.

8 Ibid.

9 As reported by Nascetti Dina. "Thou Shalt Have no Other Allah," *L'Espresso*, Dec. 5, 2003.

10 Bardot, Brigitte. *Un cri dans le silence*, Paris: Editions Le Rocher, 2003.

11 Allen, John L. "Europe's Muslims worry bishops," National Catholic Reporter, October 22, 1999.

12 Caldwell, Christopher. "Allah Mode: France's Islam Problem," *Weekly Standard*, July 15, 2002.

13 de Ravinel, Sophie. Interview with Joseph Cardinal Ratzinger, *Le Figaro*, August 13, 2004.

14 From a speech delivered at Velletri, Italy as reported by *Il Giornale del Popolo*, September 20, 2004.

15 "Villiers plaide à l'Elysée pour un référendum," *Le Figaro*, Oct. 30, 2003.

16 Cardinal Angelo Sodano made his objections known in July and September of 2002, in two memos he sent to the heads of state of the fourteen member countries then composing the EU. As reported by Sandro Magister, "Mission Impossible: Building a Church in Turkey," *L'Espresso*, Dec. 28, 2004.

17 "Saying No to Turkey," *New York Times*, Aug. 15, 2004.

18 "The New Pope," *New York Times*, April 21, 2005.

19 Bianchi, Stefania. "EU Greets Ratzinger's Election, Turkey Concerned," Inter Press Service, April 20, 2005.

20 "New Pope seen as 'anti-Turk' by Turkish press," ADN Kronos, April 20, 2005.

21 Bianchi, Stefania. "EU Greets Ratzinger's Election, Turkey Concerned," Inter Press Service, April 20, 2005.

22 Todd, Brian. "Tumult in Turkey over new pope," CNN.com, April 20, 2005.

23 D'Hippolito, Joseph. "How will Pope Benedict deal with Islam?" *Jerusalem Post*, May 8, 2005.

24 Cardinale, Gianni. "Interview with Cardinal Joseph Ratzinger: The catechism in a post-Christian world," *30 Days*, April 2003.

25 "A superior civilization? Prelate takes issue with politician's statement," *Catholic World Report*, November, 2001.

4 *The "Anti-Culture of Death"*

1 Messori, Vittorio. *The Ratzinger Report*. San Francisco: Ignatius Press, 1985.

2 Kramer, Jane. "Holy Orders," *New Yorker*, May 2, 2005.

3 Kristof, Nicholas D. "The Pope and AIDS," *New York Times*, May 8, 2005.

4 "New Pope Tries to Allay Fears of Rigid Papacy," Reuters newswire, April 20, 2005.

5 Petroff, Daniela. "Pope will not 'water down' teachings," Associated Press, May 8, 2005.

6 According to a four year study conducted by the Presidential AIDS Commission, the use of condoms resulted in a 24 percent failure rate.

In another study reported by Dr. Margaret Fishel to the International Conference on AIDS, married couples with one HIV-free partner, using condoms for protection, tested HIV + in 17% of the cases after only one and one half years (George, Marilyn. "Condom Casualties—Odds 1/6 Bedroom Roulette," AIDS Awareness News, May 12, 2000).

7 Hearst, Norman. "Condom promotion for AIDS prevention in the developing world: is it working?" *Studies in Family Planning*, March 2004.

8 Ibid.

9 Ratzinger, Joseph Cardinal. "Europe: Its Spiritual Foundations of Yesterday, Today, and Tomorrow," address at the library of the Italian Senate, Sala Capitolare del Chiostro della Minerva, May 13, 2004.

10 Mesatywa, Andiswa. "Pope: Europe corrupts Africa," News24.com South Africa, May 14, 2005.

11 "Pope warns against idolatry of riches and comfort," Catholic World News, May 4, 2005.

12 Pope Benedict XVI, Weekly catechesis, St. Peter's, May 31, 2005.

13 Stan, Adele M. "Benedict's Edicts: If you think the Catholic Church is socially dictatorial now, wait until Cardinal Ratzinger is in charge," The American Prospect, April 20, 200.

14 *The Ratzinger Report*, p. 83.

15 Ibid., p. 84.

16 Ibid., p. 85.

17 Langdon, James. "Scientists to make 'Stuart Little' mouse with the brain of a human," *London Telegraph*, March 6, 2005.

18 McVeigh, Karen. "MPs call for re-write on laws of creation," *Scotsman*, March 24, 2005.

19 *The Ratzinger Report*, p. 86.

20 De Marco, Pietro, "Remnants of Hegemony, without a Majority," *L'Espresso*, June 24, 2005.

21 "Pope Benedict XVI tries 'to protect human life'," *Pravda*, May 30, 2005.

22 "Pope angers assisted fertility campaigners in Italy," Agence France Presse, May 31, 2005.

23 Ibid.

24 Fisher, Ian and Povoledo, Elisabetta. "Benedict encourages Italy to ignore ballot," *New York Times*, May 31, 2005.

25 Ratzinger, Joseph Cardinal. "Worthiness to Receive Holy Communion—General Principles." Letter to Cardinal Theodore McCarrick and Bishop Wilton Gregory, published in *L'Espresso*, June, 2004.

26 Filteau, Jerry. "Cardinal McCarrick: No simple answers on bishop-politician relations," Catholic News Service, June 23, 2004.

5 *Expelling the Filth, Purifying the Church*

1 Ratzinger, Joseph Cardinal. "Meditations on the Way of the Cross," Roman Coliseum, Good Friday, 2005.

2 Ibid.

3 Ibid.

4 Tosatti, Marco. "Il documento che ha favorito Ratzinger," *La Stampa*, April 22, 2005.

5 Falsani, Cathleen. "George: Pope focused on scandal," *Chicago Sun-Times*, April 21, 2005.

6 "Cardinal Ratzinger Sees a Media Campaign Against Church," Zenit News Agency, December 3, 2002.

7 Goodstein, Laurie. "Pope has gained the insight to address abuse, aides say," *New York Times*, April 22, 2005.

8 Doward, Jamie. "The Pope, the letter and the child sex claim," *Observer*, April 24, 2005.

9 Ibid. Ellipses in the *Observer's* report.

10 Ibid.

11 "Houston Men Sue Pope Over Letter About Sex Abuse," Click2Houston.com, April 26, 2005.

12 Peters, Edward. "Much Ado About Not Much," *In Light of the Law*, April 27, 2005.

13 "New pope key to Vatican's response to sex-abuse scandal, says Judge Burke," Catholic News Agency, May 5, 2005.

14 Lattin, Don. "For Levada, an honor and a challenge," *San Francisco Chronicle*, May 14, 2005.

15 Levada, William J. "The San Francisco Solution," *First Things*, August/September, 1997.

16 Coleman, Gerald. "Is Proposition 22 Discriminatory?," *Valley Catholic*, Jan. 18, 2000.

17 Lattin, Don. "Levada takes heat over abuse inquiry," *San Francisco Chronicle*, Nov. 12, 2004.

18 Russell, Ron. "Settling things quietly," *S. F. Weekly*, Jan. 14-20, 2004.
19 Ibid.
20 Russell, Ron. "Bishop Bad Boy," *S. F. Weekly*, March 19, 2003.
21 Ibid.
22 Allen, John. "Word From Rome," *National Catholic Reporter*, July 22, 2005.
23 Ibid.

6 *The Invention of a "Culture of Homophobia"*

1 Congregation for the Doctrine of the Faith, "The Pastoral Care of Homosexuals," Oct. 1, 1986.
2 Sullivan, Andrew. "The Fundamentalist Triumph," The Daily Dish (andrewsullivan.com), April 19, 2005.
3 Sullivan, Andrew. "The Vicar of Orthodoxy," *Time*, April 25, 2005.
4 Bagby, Dyana. "Ratzinger strikes fear in hearts of gay Catholics," *New York Blade*, April 22, 2005.
5 Ibid.
6 Ibid.
7 GLAAD Press release, "New Pope has long, documented history of attacks on lives, families and dignity of LGBT people," April 19, 2005.
8 Jones, Susan. "Feminist, Homosexual Groups Turn Thumbs Down on New Pope," Crosswalk.com, April 20, 2005.
9 McNally, Jay. "St. Sebastian's Angels," *Catholic World Report*, October, 2001.
10 Outrage! Press release, "Cardinal Ratzinger—what do you know about his sexuality? Information sought about Vatican homophobe," April 5, 1998.
11 "Pastoral Care of Homosexuals."
12 This wording was not, however, a formulation made by Cardinal Ratzinger. He quoted the wording "intrinsically disordered" (to describe homosexual acts) from the Vatican's 1975 "Declaration on Certain Questions Concerning Sexual Ethics," wherein the subject of homosexuality was first addressed in more than a cursory way. The "homosexual condition," an inclination or desire to engage in homosexual acts, was not addressed in the 1975 document. Cardinal Ratzinger made a point in the 1986 document to clarify that the "homosexual condition," although distinct from and different from homosexual acts themselves, is also

"intrinsically disordered," although neither immoral or evil in itself.

13 "Pastoral Care of Homosexuals."

14 Marech, Rona. "Many gay Catholics disappointed with cardinals' choice for pope, seeing Ratzinger as church's most outspoken foe of equal rights," April 20, 2005.

15 Ibid.

16 Ibid.

17 Congregation for the Doctrine of the Faith, "Some considerations on legislation prohibiting discrimination against homosexual persons," July 23, 1992.

18 Congregation for the Doctrine of the Faith, "Considerations Regarding Proposals to Give Legal Recognition to Unions Between Homosexual Persons," July, 2003.

19 Withers, James. "Catholics commiserate: New York's gay Roman Catholics pray for justice," *New York Blade*, April 29, 2005.

20 Feyernick, Deborah. "Cardinal O'Connor remembered as 'moral compass'," Associated Press, May 4, 2000.

21 "An Enlightened Church: Letters to Young Catholics," *Conscience* (newsletter of Catholics for a Free Choice), Summer, 2002.

22 Congregation for the Doctrine of the Faith, "Notification regarding Sister Jeannine Gramick, SSND, and Father Robert Nugent, SDS," May 31, 1999.

23 Nugent, Robert and Jeannine Gramick. *Building bridges: Gay and lesbian reality and the Catholic Church*, New York: Twenty-Third Publications, 1992.

24 Article 23-27: *Acta Apostolicae Sedis* 89, 1997, CDF.

25 Congregation for the Doctrine of the Faith, "Notification regarding Sister Jeannine Gramick, SSND, and Father Robert Nugent, SDS," May 31, 1999.

26 "Response of Sister Jeannine Gramick, SSND to the Congregation for the Doctrine of the Faith regarding Erroneous and Dangerous Propositions in the Publications 'Building Bridges' and 'Voices of Hope'," Feb. 5, 1998.

27 Congregation for the Doctrine of the Faith, "Notification regarding Sister Jeannine Gramick, SSND, and Father Robert Nugent, SDS, July 13, 1999.

28 Ibid.

29 Coleman, Gerald. "Ministry to Homosexuals Must Use Authentic Church Teaching," *America*, August 14-21, 1999.

30 "Statement of Fr. Robert Nugent, SDS," July 14, 1999.

31 "U.S. Nun Bemoans New Pope," Associated Press, April 19, 2005.

7 *Insisting Upon Sound Doctrine*

1 Ratzinger, Joseph Cardinal. Address to the Tenth Synod of Bishops, October 6, 2001.

2 Congregation for the Doctrine of the Faith, "Instruction on Certain Aspects of the Theology of Liberation," August, 1984.

3 Ratzinger, Joseph Cardinal. "Relativism: The Central Problem for Faith Today," address to the presidents of the Doctrinal Commissions of the Bishops' Conferences of Latin America, Guadalajara, Mexico, May, 1996.

4 Knitter, Paul. Preface by Hans Kung, *One Earth Many Religions: Multifaith Dialogue & Global Responsibility*, New York: Orbis Books, 1995.

5 Ibid., p. 3.

6 Ibid., p. 5.

7 Ibid., p. 6.

8 Knitter, Paul F. *No Other Name: A Critical Survey of Christian Attitudes Toward the World Religions*. New York: Orbis Books, 1985.

9 Ibid.

10 Knitter, Paul F. and Hick, John. *The Myth of Christian Uniqueness: Toward a Pluralistic Theology of Religions*. New York: Orbis Books, 1988.

11 Ibid.

12 Knitter, Paul. *One Earth Many Religions*, p. 9.

13 Ibid., p. 10.

14 Ibid., p. 13.

15 Ibid., p.15.

16 Hill, Brennan, Knitter, Paul, and Madges, William. Faith, *Relgion & Theology: A Contemporary Introduction*, Mystic CT: Twenty-Third Publications, Revised edition, 1997.

17 Dupuis, Jacques. *Toward a Christian Theology of Religious Pluralism*, New York: Orbis Books, 1999 (English-language edition).

18 Congregation for the Doctrine of the Faith, "Notification relative to the book of Jacques Dupuis, *Toward a Christian Theology of Religious Pluralism*," Jan. 24, 2001.

19 "Obit: Father Jacques Dupuis: Jesuit theologian whose experience in India underpinned his challenging views on interfaith dialogue," *London Times*, Jan. 12, 2005.
20 Congregation for the Doctrine of the Faith, "Notification concerning the text *Mary and Human Liberation* by Fr. Tissa Balasuriya, O.M.I.," January 2, 1997.
21 Congregation for the Doctrine of the Faith, "Notification concerning the writings of Father Anthony De Mello, SJ," June 24, 1998.
22 Allen, John L. "Two more scholars censured by Rome," *National Catholic Reporter*, March 1, 2002.
23 Ibid.
24 Funk, Robert W. *The Five Gospels: The Search for the Authentic Words of Jesus*, HarperSanFrancisco; Reprint edition, 1997.
25 Ratzinger, Joseph Cardinal. Address to the Tenth Synod of Bishops, October 6, 2001.
26 "Activists for Roman Catholic women voice fears over new pope," *Hindustan Times*, April 20, 2005.
27 Ibid.
28 "'The Great Inquisitor' and His Critics," *Deutsche Welle*, April 21, 2005.

8 *Remodeling the Face of the Church*

1 Ratzinger, Joseph Cardinal. *Milestones: Memoirs 1927-1977*, San Francisco: Ignatius Press, 1998 (English translation).
2 Ibid.
3 Allen, John L. "In rare U.S. visit, Ratzinger urges scholars to 'think with the church'," *National Catholic Reporter*, Feb. 26, 2005.
4 Ibid.
5 Gamber, Klaus. Introduction by Joseph Cardinal Ratzinger. *The Reform of the Roman Liturgy*, Boulder CO: Roman Catholic Books, 1993.
6 Ratzinger. *Milestones*.
7 Ibid.
8 Ibid.
9 Ibid.
10 Ratzinger, Joseph Cardinal. "The Organic Development of the Liturgy," *30 Days*, December, 2004.
11 Ibid.

12 Ratzinger, Joseph Cardinal. *Spirit of the Liturgy*, San Francisco: Ignatius Press, 2000 (English-language edition).
13 Ibid.
14 Ibid.
15 Ratzinger. "The Organic Development of the Liturgy."
16 Ibid.
17 Ibid.
18 Ibid.
19 Allen, John L. "Identity Politics in Switzerland; The Vatican and America; Personnel Changes in the Holy See; Bonhoeffer and Ratzinger," *National Catholic Reporter*, June 11, 2004.
20 Magister, Sandro. "The 'Reform of the Reform' Has Already Begun," *L'Espresso*, April 28, 2005.
21 Ferrara, Christopher. "Good News and Bad—Already," *Remnant*, April 20, 2005 (online edition).
22 McCaffery, Roger. "What Sort of Man is This?" *Seattle Catholic*, May 5, 2005.
23 Ratzinger, Joseph Cardinal. "Ten Years of the Motu Proprio 'Ecclesia Dei'," (English translation by Fr. Ignatius Harrison), Ergife Palace Hotel, Rome, October 24, 1998.
24 Davies, Michael. "The Pontifical Mass of Cardinal Ratzinger in Weimer," Una Voce International.
25 Fellay, Bernard. "SSPX Press Communique: On the election of Pope Benedict XVI," April 19, 2005.
26 Magister, Sandro. "Benedict XVI: The Pope and His Agenda," *L'Espresso*, April 20, 2005.

9 *Shedding the "Armor of Saul"*

1 Form a letter sent to Archbishop Raymond Hunthausen, September 30, 1985 and published in The Progress, the diocesan newspaper for the Archdiocese of Seattle, on May 28, 1987.
2 Ratzinger, Joseph Cardinal. *A New Song for the Lord: Faith in Christ and the Liturgy Today*, New York: Crossroads Publishing Company, 1996.
3 Magister. "Benedict XVI: The Pope and His Agenda".
4 Weigel, George. *Witness to Hope: The Biography of Pope John Paul II*, New York: HarperCollins, 1999.

5 Archbishop Jadot fell out of favor with the Vatican of John Paul II. On June 27, 1980, was pulled out of Washington and given the Vatican post of "Pro-President of Non-Christians."

6 Wheeler, Jack. "The De-Homosexualization of the Catholic Church," *To the Point*, April 26, 2005.

7 Sobran, Joseph. "Bishop in the Doghouse," *National Review*, Dec. 19, 1986.

8 Form a letter sent to Archbishop Raymond Hunthausen, September 30, 1985 and published in *The Progress*, the diocesan newspaper for the Archdiocese of Seattle, on May 28, 1987.

9 Ibid.

10 Ibid.

11 Bullert, Gary. *The Hunthausen File,* Seattle: St. Thomas League, 1992, p. 65.

12 Sobran, Joseph. "Bishop in the Doghouse," *National Review*, Dec. 19, 1986.

13 Ibid.

14 Letter to the Editor, *National Catholic Reporter*, October 23, 1986.

15 Sobran, Joseph. "Bishop in the Doghouse," *National Review*, Dec. 19, 1986.

16 Bullert, Gary. The Hunthausen File.

17 Ibid.

18 Tu, Janet. "Local Catholics split on choice of pope," *Seattle Times*, April 20, 2005.

19 Roberts, Tom and Allen, John L. "Editor of Jesuits' *America* magazine forced to resign under Vatican pressure," *National Catholic Reporter* Online, May 6, 2005.

20 "Scandal at America," *Commonweal*, May 6, 2005.

21 Neuhaus, Richard John. "Thinking With the Church," *Boston Globe*, May 16, 2005.

22 Ibid.

A NOTE ON THE AUTHOR

MICHAEL S. ROSE, the author of the *New York Times* bestseller *Goodbye, Good Men*, is famous for his penetrating and reliable coverage of the Catholic Church. Educated at Brown University and the University of Cincinnati, he has written five previous books and is the Web Editor of the *New Oxford Review*. Mr Rose's work has appeared in the *Wall Street Journal*, *New York Newsday*, the *American Conservative*, and *Catholic World Report*. He is married with five children.

This book was designed and set into type
by Mitchell S. Muncy,
with cover design by Stephen J. Ott,
and printed and bound
by Bang Printing,
Brainerd, Minnesota.

❦

The text face is Minion Multiple Master,
designed by Robert Slimbach
and issued in digital form by Adobe Systems,
Mountain View, California, in 1991.

❦

The paper is acid-free and is of archival quality.